IMAGES
*of America*

# BROCTON AND PORTLAND

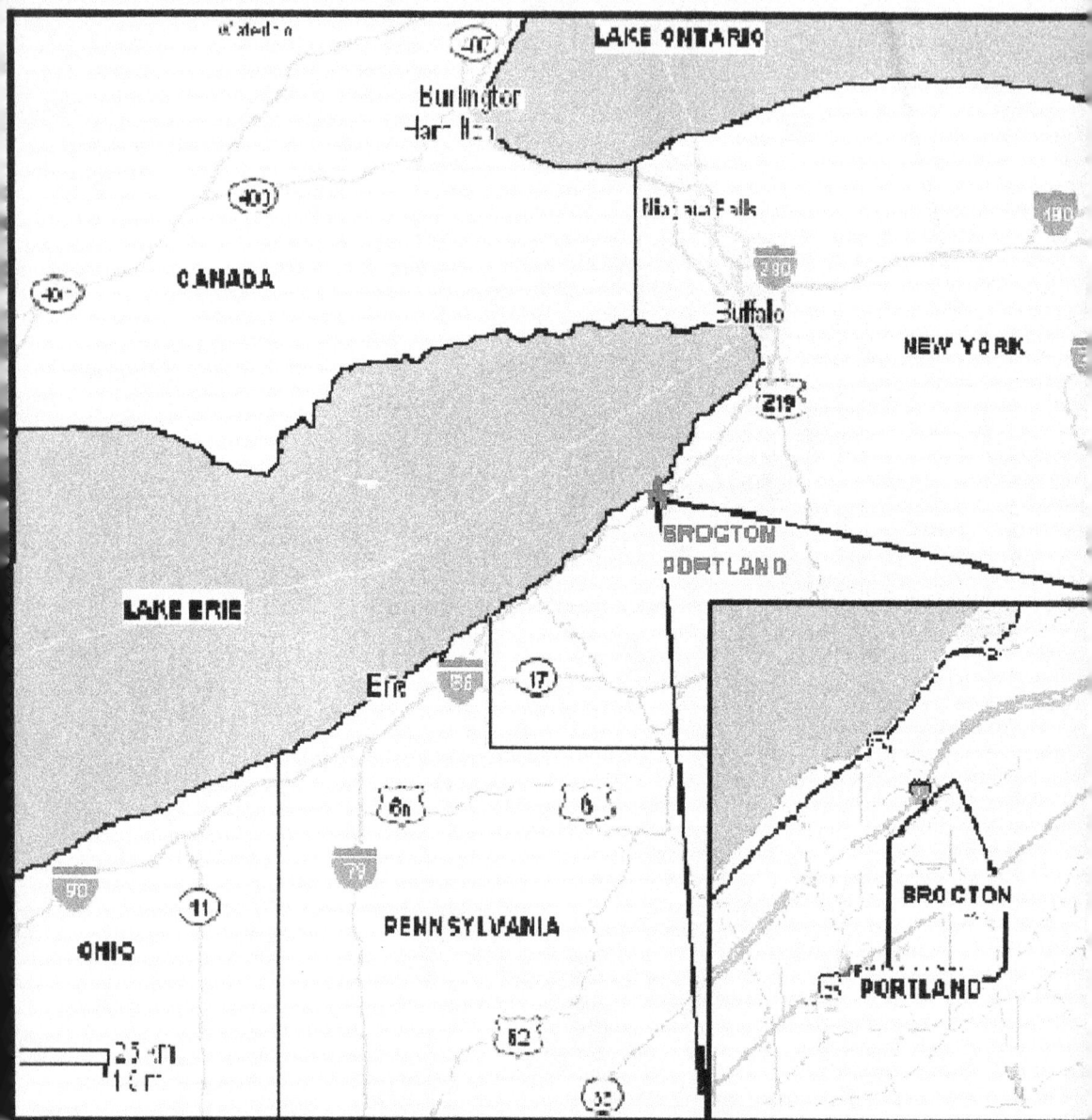

This map shows the location of the town of Portland and the village of Brocton along the Lake Erie shoreline. (Courtesy of George Kurtz.)

*On the cover*: This 1913 photograph was taken during the construction of the Brocton arch that was erected for Portland's centennial celebration. (Courtesy of Belden Photo.)

IMAGES
*of America*

# BROCTON AND PORTLAND

Edward T. Kurtz Sr.

ARCADIA
PUBLISHING

Published by Arcadia Publishing
Charleston SC, Chicago IL, Portsmouth NH, San Francisco CA


Library of Congress Catalog Card Number: 2006938008

For all general information contact Arcadia Publishing at:
Telephone 843-853-2070
Fax 843-853-0044
E-mail sales@arcadiapublishing.com
For customer service and orders:
Toll-Free 1-888-313-2665

Visit us on the Internet at www.arcadiapublishing.com

*Dedicated to Elias and Anita Kurtz and Edgar and Roberta Judge.*

# CONTENTS

# ACKNOWLEDGMENTS

This project's acknowledgment begins with the historical pride that my father, who became both the town of Portland's historian as well as the village of Brocton's historian, instilled in me as a young man growing up in the town. As a young adult, he made me aware of the importance of the surrounding historical places and structures in the community. For this, I will forever be grateful.

I would like to give a special thanks to my wife who has endured and encouraged my love and pursuit of local history and has greatly aided me in putting together this book. I also give a special thanks to my youngest son, George, who has also helped me with this project.

A thank you goes out to John Slater of Niagara Falls, who started me on this project. Another thank you goes to Kirk Bennett, who helped with extra photographs needed to fill in the gaps of my collection.

Special thanks are given to Elias Kurtz, a Brocton historian who wrote important notes between 1960 and 1980.

Finally thank you to my editor, Pam O'Neil, of Arcadia Publishing, for her help, guidance, and patience with me in the process, and also to Arcadia Publishing for allowing me to put forth this book.

# INTRODUCTION

In the year 1804, a young man from Meadville, Pennsylvania, was seen traveling about what is now the town of Portland with his dog, surveying the land, and searching for property that would be suitable for his family's home in the unsettled land of western New York State. In the summer of 1804, James Dunn found and cleared a small plot of land, made arrangements to buy 1,000 acres, and returned to Meadville for his family. He again returned in 1805 and started to build his new home in the wilds of western New York State. Dunn was the first settler of Portland. He was not to be the last, as by the year 1812, 38 more families had settled in Portland. Today, 200 years later, Portland is still a rural community.

Dunn was interested in the education of not only his children but of all the pioneer families. He was responsible for setting up the first schools in Portland as well as an exchange library to encourage reading.

By 1836, Deacon Elijah Fay had introduced the growing of grapes to Portland. The grape juice was made into wine to be used for communion and by doctors for medicinal purposes.

The Concord grape was first introduced in 1859. The growing grapes in western New York State was about to become a major industry involving not only grape farming but also associated industries such as railroads for shipping the grapes and wine making.

As the 20th century progressed, the town did well surviving the hard times of the Depression. During the last half of the century, the grape industry changed and so did the town—from one largely dependent on the grape industry to a bedroom community with a couple of light industries and residents traveling to nearby cities for work.

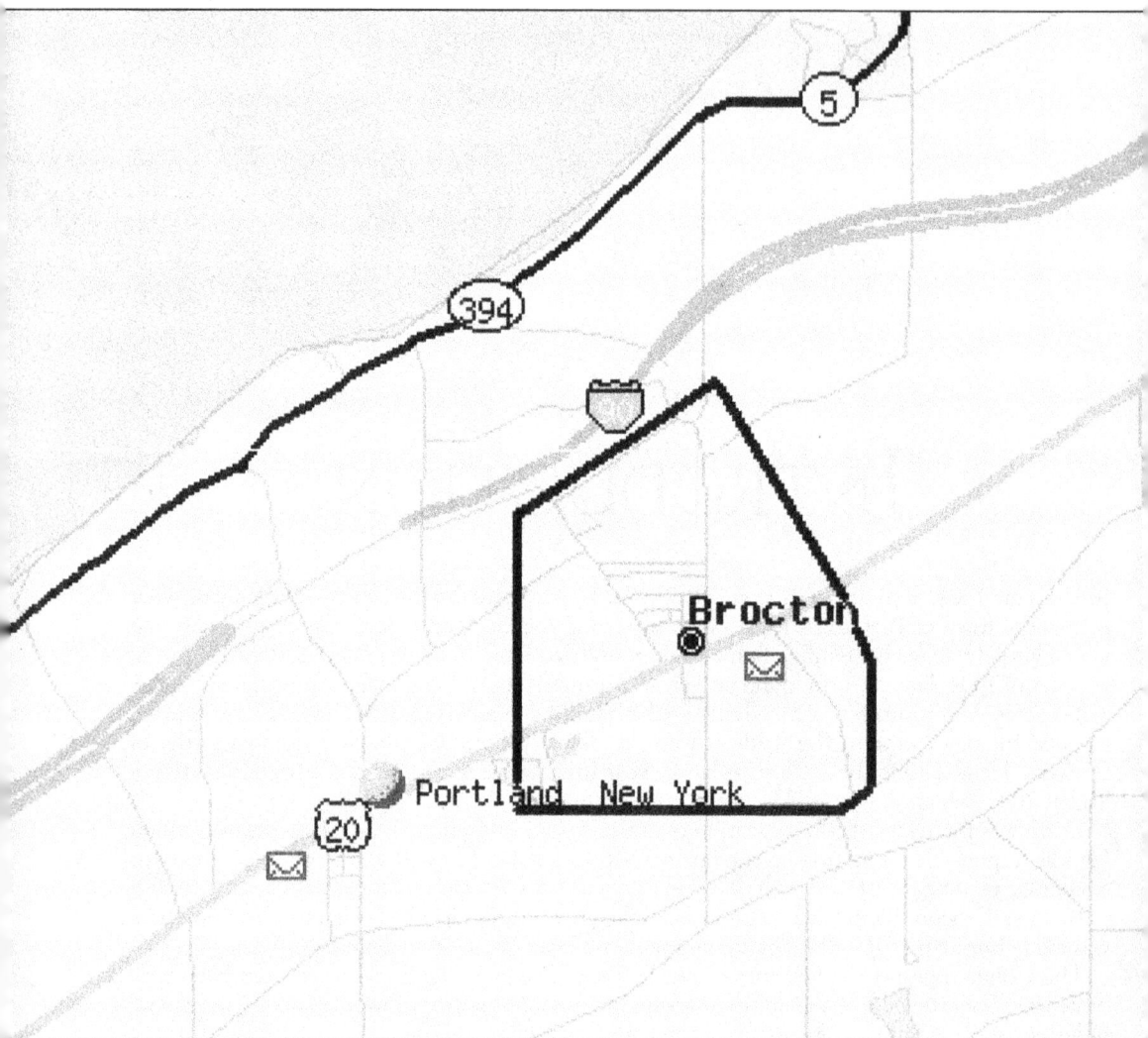

This shows residential maps of Portland and Brocton and the location of Brocton in comparison to the surrounding area of western New York. (Courtesy of George Kurtz.)

# One

# PORTLAND HAMLET AND CENTERVILLE

The hamlet of Portland was, for its early years, a vast wooded area. As families moved in, more businesses and services were needed and the hamlet that was Portland Center, or Centerville, was formed.

At first, there were just a few essential services. Among the occupations available were farmer, merchant, saddler, and mechanic, as well as a hotel proprietor and tavern keeper. Several churches were also established.

The Portland Post Office was established on December 7, 1814, and Calvin Barnes was appointed the postmaster. The office was first in his log home, then it moved to a frame house at the forks of old Erie Road, which is today Ellicott Road. He remained postmaster for 15 years until the post office was closed due to political and controversial newspaper matter. North Portland Post Office was established in 1828 and located at a tavern east of the present village of Brocton by its appointed postmaster, Moses Sage. In 1830, Sage moved to Fredonia. He then moved the post office to a tavern west of Brocton owned by John R. Conley. Conley was appointed postmaster on September 3, 1830, and the office name was changed to Portland. In 1835, Conley moved the office to a tavern house he built in Centerville or Portland Center. It has changed buildings several times but remains in the hamlet.

The hamlet was never officially named Centerville. Due to its central location, the name was adopted by many town residents during the mid- to late 1800s. Today people refer to it as the hamlet of Portland.

The hamlet of Portland never reached the growth of its nearby neighbors, the village of Brocton and the village of Westfield. This small hamlet is still made up of a few small businesses, a community church, and a post office.

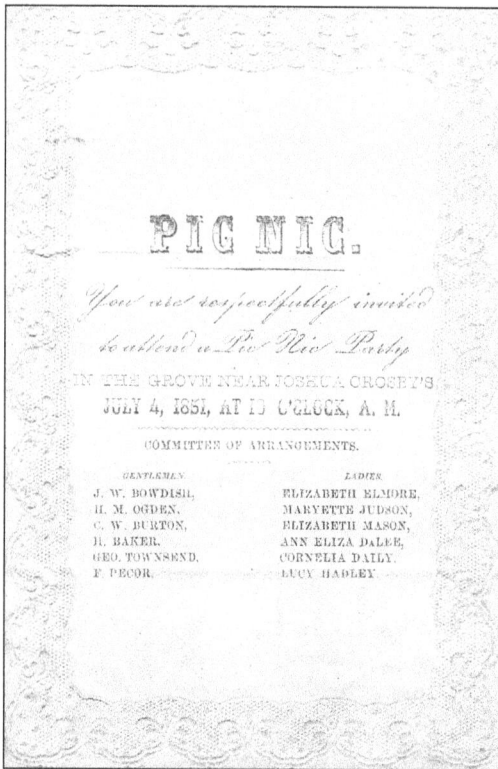

Summertime in Centerville enabled residents to enjoy good food and friendship at Fourth of July celebrations. Invitations to a "pig nic," in the grove near Joshua Crosby's house, were received by many town residents in 1851.

## PIG NIC.

You are respectfully invited to attend a Pic Nic Party
IN THE GROVE NEAR JOSHUA CROSBY'S,
JULY 4, 1851, AT 10 O'CLOCK, A. M.

COMMITTEE OF ARRANGEMENTS.

| GENTLEMEN. | LADIES. |
|---|---|
| J. W. BOWDISH, | ELIZABETH ELMORE, |
| H. M. OGDEN, | MARYETTE JUDSON, |
| C. W. BURTON, | ELIZABETH MASON, |
| H. BAKER, | ANN ELIZA DALEE, |
| GEO. TOWNSEND, | CORNELIA DAILY, |
| F. PECOR, | LUCY HADLEY. |

Independence Day dances were also a very popular social gathering. This is an invitation to attend an Independence Day dance at the Union Hotel in Centerville on Monday, July 4, 1859, at 7:00 p.m. The managers of the dance were all prominent families of early Portland. The invitation was printed on linen paper with an embossed floral design around the edges.

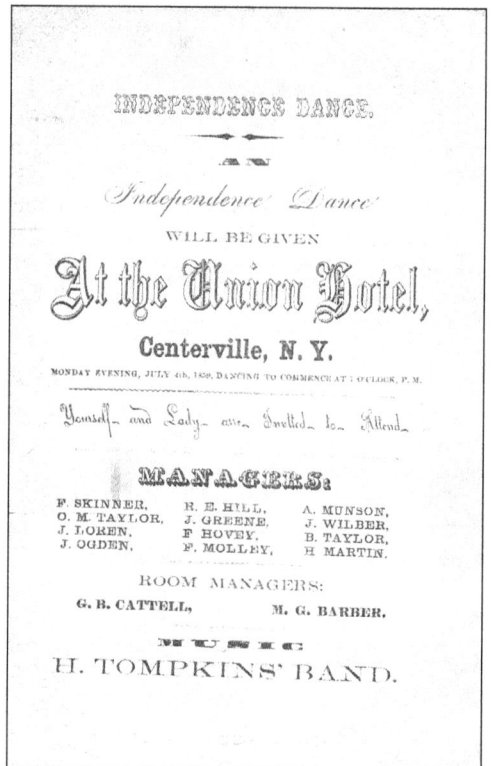

### INDEPENDENCE DANCE.

Independence Dance
WILL BE GIVEN
At the Union Hotel,
Centerville, N. Y.
MONDAY EVENING, JULY 4th, 1859, DANCING TO COMMENCE AT 7 O'CLOCK, P. M.

Yourself and Lady are invited to attend.

#### MANAGERS:

| F. SKINNER, | R. E. HILL, | A. MUNSON, |
|---|---|---|
| O. M. TAYLOR, | J. GREENE, | J. WILBER, |
| J. LOREN, | F HOVEY, | B. TAYLOR, |
| J. OGDEN, | F. MOLLEY, | H MARTIN. |

ROOM MANAGERS:

G. B. CATTELL,          M. G. BARBER.

MUSIC
H. TOMPKINS' BAND.

Early settlers of Centerville looked forward to social events. This is an invitation to attend a dance to celebrate the opening of the Union Hotel in Centerville on April 23, 1855. Tomkin's Band performed for the attendees' enjoyment.

Social events were not always held on the weekend. This invitation to attend a social dance was held on Wednesday, May 17, 1856. Again the Tomkin's Band provided the music at the Union Hotel in Centerville. Note that the date was changed from May 8 to May 17.

11

This postcard, postmarked in 1907, shows the Union Hotel with its name changed to the Portland Inn. The concrete block building was located on the corner of Main and Fay Streets and was then owned by Charles Orone. It burned down in 1933. The neighbor, Mrs. Titus, discovered flames coming from the third floor and woke up the family who was sleeping on the second floor. Brocton and Fredonia fire companies were called but by the time they got to the building, it was too late to save. The owners were said to have had $7,500 insurance on the building and $1,000 on its contents.

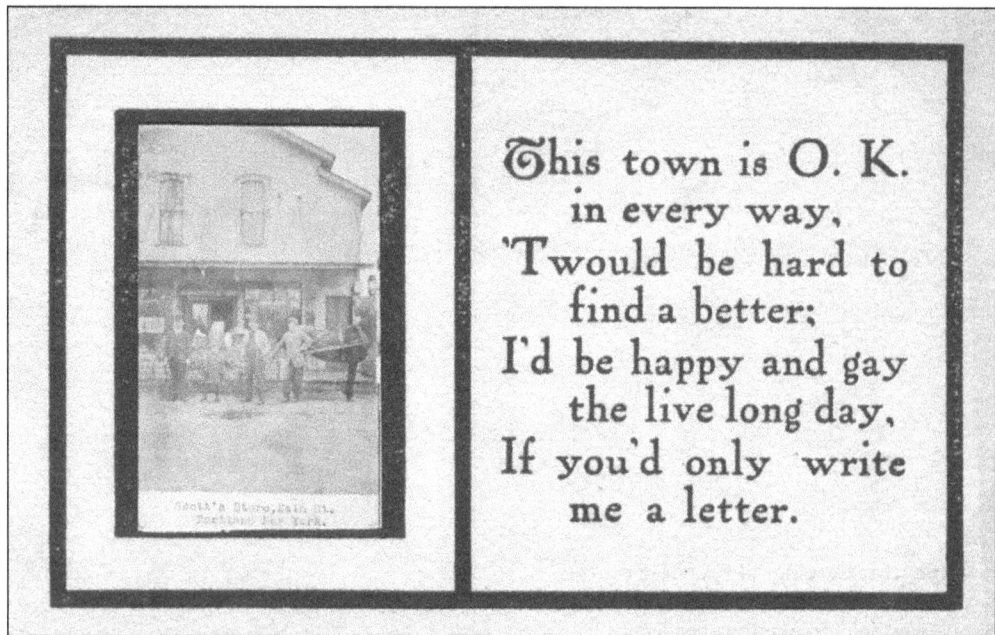

This town is O. K.
in every way,
'Twould be hard to
find a better;
I'd be happy and gay
the live long day,
If you'd only write
me a letter.

Postcards were made and sold in local businesses. This card, which dates from around 1910, shows a small photograph of Scott's Store on Main Street in Portland, but also has a nice verse requesting a letter to the sender.

12

This real-photo postcard dates from the early 1900s and shows Main Street in the hamlet of Portland, looking east. All roads were dirt. Church Street turns from Main Street on the left side of the photograph. Scott's Store is on the left side where the horse and buckboard are shown. Note the trolley car tracks in the middle of the road and the woman standing in front of the house on the corner of Church and Main Streets. The hamlet's character has not changed much since this photograph was taken except for a few trees removed, roads paved, and wire poles changed.

Winters were harsh in Portland. This real-photo postcard is looking east toward Brocton along Main Street (Route 20) from the intersection of Fay and Pecor Streets. The snow on the trees is so picturesque. This picture was taken around 1910.

This photograph shows a busy Scott's Store in the hamlet of Portland during the early 1900s. J. F. Scott is standing in the center of the photograph with patrons of his store. Mrs. Scott and their dog are standing on the front porch at the left. At the present time, this building holds apartments and the Portland Post Office.

## INVITATION DANCE

given by

## Lake Shore Camp, 3, Woodmen of the World

Star Hotel, Portland, N. Y.

## FRIDAY EVENING, NOVEMBER 12, 1909

Round and Square Dances        Music by Skinner's Orchestra

TICKETS PER COUPLE 50 CENTS

**PRESENT THIS INVITATION AT THE DOOR**

As time passed, socials remained very important to the residents. This is an invitation to attend a dance given by Lake Shore Camp, 3, Woodman of the World. It was held at the Star Hotel in Portland on Friday, November 12, 1909. The Skinner Orchestra provided the music. The cost for tickets was 50¢ per couple.

As automobiles became available, gasoline products were considered essential goods. This is a real-photo postcard of Burn's Cash Store, on Main Street in Portland, dated 1926. The store was on the south side of Route 20 in the center of the hamlet. Note the gas pump out front and the sign selling Socony motor oils. This building later housed the post office for a short time, then an antique shop, and now a liquor store.

In the late 1800s, R. D. Fuller and W. G. Skinner founded the Portland Wine Cellars, proprietors of wines and brandies. The business was located in the hotel owned by Fuller. This building was located on the north side of Main Street in the middle of the business district. In modern times, this building became known as the Oasis Bar and Grill. The building burned down in 2002. This photograph shows Avery Burton proudly holding the horse and carriage in which W. G. Skinner and R. D. Fuller are sitting.

Grape growing and harvesting was very important business for Portland residents. This grape label from the late 1800s was placed on each 12-quart basket of Concord grapes that were packed for the Morse Star Brand. The packer was E. D. Morse.

Some years, the grape harvest is better and larger than other years. This real-photo postcard that was postmarked in 1914 shows the front of the Morse grape packing barn that was located on West Main Street just west of the center of the hamlet. The number of crates and baskets and the notation on the back of card indicate that 1914 was a very good year for the grape harvest.

Men, women, and children helped with the grape harvest. This postcard that was postmarked in 1912 shows two women in the grape vineyard hand picking the grapes. The weather must have been warm because the women are in light clothing and are wearing hats.

This postmarked envelope from Portland shows a January 28, 1881, cancellation from the Portland Post Office. This star cancel post marking is very rare. The Portland Post Office used this star cancel in 1881 and 1882.

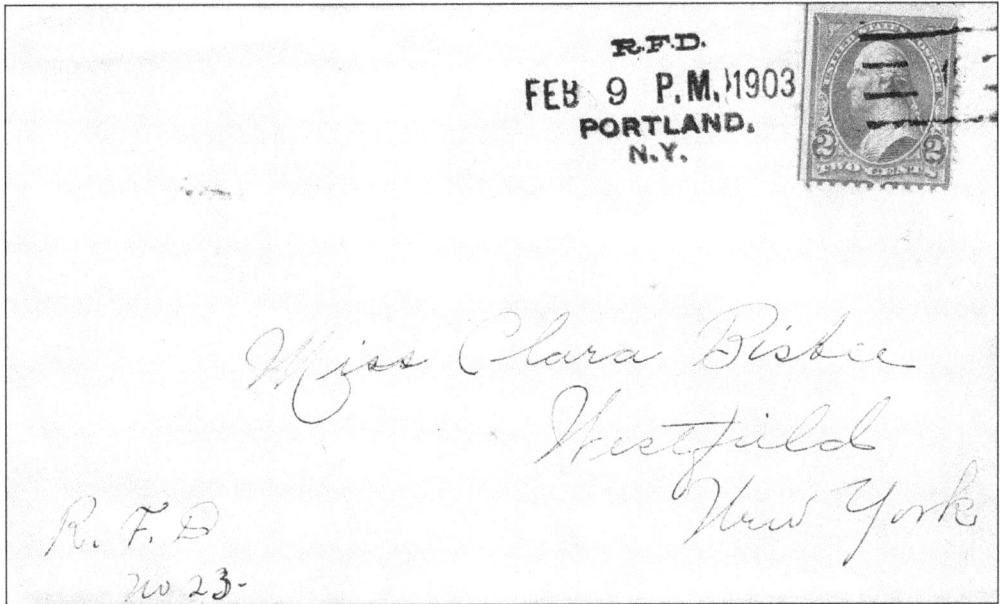

R.F.D.
FEB 9 P.M. 1903
PORTLAND,
N.Y.

*Miss Clara Bishee*
*Westfield*
*New York*

*R. F. D*
*no 23 -*

Rural Free Delivery (RFD) cancels were frequently found in rural towns. These RFD cancellations were replaced by modern methods. This postmarked February 9, 1903, RFD Portland envelope is a nice example.

CO. U.S. ARMY, PORTLAND N.Y.

Not only were men from Portland called to duty in the armed forces, soldiers came to Portland as well. This real-photo postcard was taken around 1917 and shows a U.S. Army company in Portland. They are on West Main Street, about one mile west of the hamlet marching east. It is not known where their destination was but it is presumed that they were on a training drill getting ready to go overseas during World War I.

New modes of transportation called for modern road technology. This postcard from about 1906 shows the Overhead Bridge over the Pennsylvania Railroad on what is now Route 20, which connected the hamlet of Portland with its eastern neighbor, the village of Brocton. This major roadway was used not only by horse and buggy but also by the streetcar line. The railroad abandoned the tracks in the 1980s. The State of New York then removed the bridge.

Vincent C. Woodruff was an enterprising man. Two miles west of the hamlet of Portland along Main Street, Woodruff started a retail business called the Tent. This 1921 advertising postcard shows a 1910 Model T Ford that was owned and operated by Woodruff for several years and could be found at the Tent on Route 20.

Overhead Bridge, Portland, N. Y.

If one was not fortunate enough to own an automobile in the early 1900s, one could ride a trolley or streetcar to a destination. This postcard shows a Buffalo and Lake Erie Traction Company streetcar, which serviced the town, heading west along Route 20 toward Portland on the Overhead Bridge.

BUFFALO & LAKE ERIE
TRACTION CO.

PORTLAND

GOING)     —TO—     (COUPON

WESTFIELD

CONTINUOUS PASSAGE ONLY.
NOT GOOD IF DETACHED.

BUFFALO & LAKE ERIE
TRACTION CO.

WESTFIELD

RETURN)     —TO—     (COUPON

PORTLAND

Continuous Passage
only.
                    General Manager.

Buffalo & Lake Erie Traction Co.

GOOD FOR ONE CONTINUOUS
FIVE CENT RIDE ON ANY LINE OF
THIS COMPANY.
Form CF 294

678056          Gen'l Mgr.

Here is a c. 1918 round-trip ticket from Portland, to Westfield, and back again on the Buffalo and Lake Erie Traction Company. The other ticket shown is from about 1920 and is good for one continuous 5¢ ride on any line of the Buffalo and Lake Erie Traction Company.

Portland had several general merchandise stores in the early 1900s. Here are three receipts from stores in the hamlet. Scott's Store was on West Main Street. This receipt shows that the customer purchased mantle globes and also paid her $147.61 bill in full. A. D. Titus's store was located east of the Methodist Church on Main Street. Mr. Walters purchased a watch for $2. C. C. Burr, dealer in general hardware, also had a store in the hamlet. Mr. Cranberg purchased a variety of items including a coffee pot for a total of $1.63.

# Two

# PROSPECT STATION

Prospect Station lies in the southwest portion of the town. In 1865, a railroad named the Oil Creek Crosscut Railroad ran between Corry, Pennsylvania, and Brocton, where it joined the Buffalo and Erie Railroad. Trains going north or south needed a place to stop on their way to Corry. The intersection of Fish and Barnes Roads was chosen, and the spot was then named Prospect Station. Soon after its establishment, a depot station with a restaurant, a hotel, a general store, a tavern, and a post office followed. In the late 1880s, it also became a shipping station for local grape growers. By the early 1900s, when there was more modern railroad technology, the railroad stop at Prospect Station was no longer needed and was abandoned. Soon after, Prospect Station became a ghost town. A few foundations still remain as a reminder of this once-prosperous spot in town.

Alpha Barnes was appointed postmaster of Prospect Station on December 9, 1868. The post office was discontinued in 1910 and Westfield took over its service.

On Christmas Eve in 1872, Portland's worst train disaster occurred at Prospect Station. There was a 25-foot-high trestle that trains had to use in order to go up the hill toward Prospect Station. At 2:30 in the afternoon on that Christmas Eve, a mail train with an engine, a tender, a baggage car, and a passenger car with 50 people was slowly heading down the hill when it encountered work being done on the trestle. The engineer tried to stop but could not. It was just enough of a bump that the flange on the rear left wheel of the tender broke, causing the tender itself, the baggage car, and the full passenger car to fall over the trestle into the gulf that was 25 feet below. Shortly after landing in the gulf, the passenger car caught fire. The brakeman, who had jumped clear from the car as it was falling, ran a half mile to Prospect Station for help. By the time he got back to the wreck, neighbors and survivors had arrived and tried to help the wounded. For many passengers it was too late. Twenty people died from this tragedy.

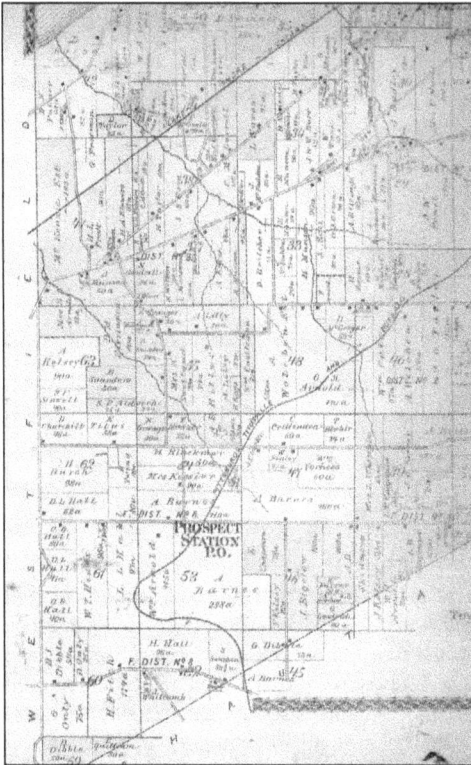

This is a map from the 1867 *Chautauqua County Atlas* showing the location of Prospect Station. As one can see, Alpha Barnes owned over 500 acres of land at Prospect Station. William Arnold owned 115 acres of land near where the fateful railroad trestle was located. In the testimony concerning the accident, the brakeman testified the daughter of Arnold was considered a hero for the help that she gave the injured caused from the accident.

"FENTON LIGHT ROADSTER."

## Bicycles and Sundres:

My line of bicycles and sundries for 1894 are the best that money can buy. My entire line of bicycles will be sold only at list price to all. If you buy a wheel of me and pay $125, you will know that your neighbor cannot buy the same wheel for one cent less. Fenton's weight 19 to 32 pounds; $160 to $125. New Mail, weight 26 to 30 pounds; price $125 to $115. Emblems, 25 to 31 pounds, with the M. & W. pneumatic tire; price $100 to $55. I will make it to your interest to deal with me. Agents wanted in unoccupied territory. I have second-hand wheels from $15 to $30. Send for my catalogue.

JOHN MAWHIR, Prospect Station, N. Y.

John Mawhir owned land at Prospect Station. When the railroad was constructed and a post office was established, Mawhir opened a Bicycle and Sundries Store. This is an 1894 advertisement for the Fenton Light Roadster. It appears that bicycles were costly.

Although the railroad station was busy at times, the railway agent had time to rest. The agent is standing in the doorway of Prospect Station. The sign next to the door partially reads American Express.

Prospect Station Ghost Town

Traveling from Brocton south, trains had to traverse a grade of over 5 degrees for nearly 8 miles. They had to be light to make the climb, and had to stop for water and wood on top of the hill. The place chosen for the stop was the intersection of Fish and Barnes Roads and the name chosen was Prospect Station.

A railroad depot was built here, circa 1865, allowing trains to load firewood and water. Soon a hotel, general store and post office was established, and prospered for 40 years. Prospect Station closed around 1910, after train engines changed and no longer needed to stop.

As one can see in this recent photograph, Prospect Station is now considered a ghost town. There is a hiking trail along the railroad bed and visitors can see foundations of buildings once inhabited by businesses and people who had high hopes of maintaining a busy community. However, that is all that remains to this small but important part of Portland. (Courtesy of George Kurtz.)

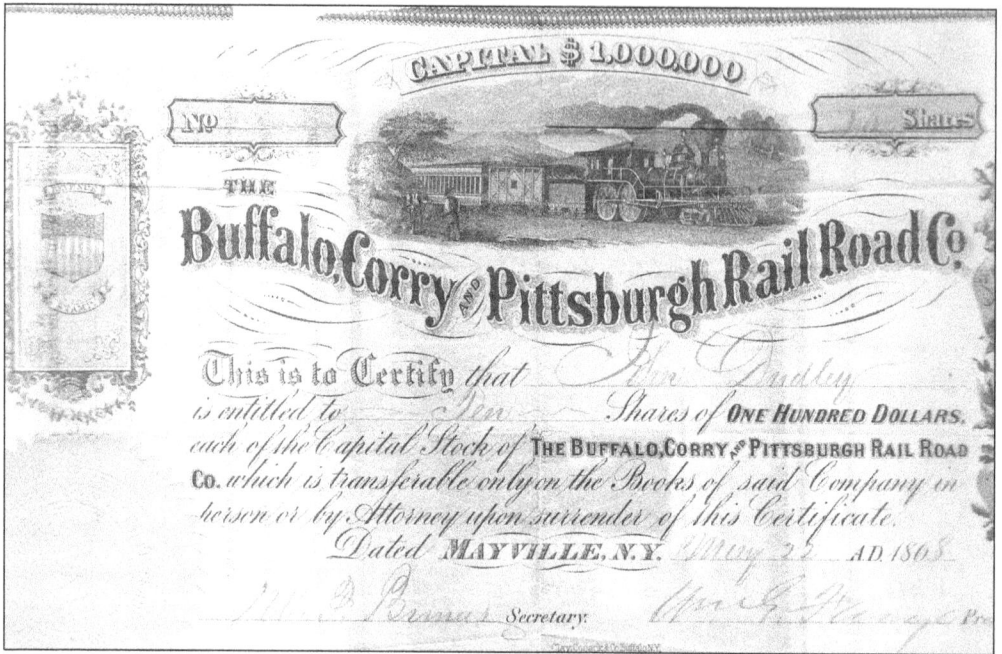

Capital was needed to make the Buffalo, Corry and Pittsburgh Railroad Company successful. This is the No. 12 certificate for 10 shares at $100 each of capital stock for the railroad company. John Dudley purchased these shares May 22, 1868. They were filed in Mayville, the county seat.

Though Prospect Station no longer exists, there is a business nearby. Vetter Vineyards Winery produces a variety of quality wines. The mailing address is 8005 Prospect Station Road in Westfield. Here are two of their labels for pinot grigio and riesling. Besides grapes, local blueberries are used to make delicious blueberry wine and blueberry port. This is the only winery in the town of Portland.

# *Three*

# BROCTON AND SALEM CROSS ROADS

Brocton is currently an incorporated village with some 1,200 residents. In its heyday, however, it was a bustling place with many businesses and residents. Railroad entrepreneur George Pullman and Washington Senators pitcher Eddie Matteson were both born in Brocton, and the cartoon character Marmaduke was created here by Portland native Brad Anderson.

In early times the land was swampy, and Slippery Rock Creek ran through the center. Some 24 log and frame dwellings stood on the outskirts of the present-day business district. The villagers wanted their own post office after hearing that one was going to be established in Portland. They attended a meeting at Landais Lathrop's shop, where they each wrote down a suggested name for the village. The name that was drawn from the hat was Salem, which could not be used since a post office with that name already existed. In 1834, the name Salem Cross Roads was adopted, and shortly afterward a post office was established.

By 1857, railroads and hotels were serving Salem Cross Roads. Hotel owners Mr. Brockway and James Minton got together, took the first four letters of Brockway and the last three letters of Minton, and coined the name Brocton. On September 7, 1857, the post office and the village were renamed Brocton.

On March 20, 1894, the villagers voted 127 to 60 in favor of incorporation. Brocton began to boom. Main Street was widened, and streetlamps and sidewalks were added. New businesses were established, including a three-story State Bank of Brocton and the Brocton House Hotel. In 1896, a new Western New York and Pennsylvania Railroad station was opened, a municipal water system was established, and the first two fire departments—Brocton Hose Company and Citizens Hose Company No. 1—were formed. The Portland Telephone Company was established in 1898. By the early 1900s, a power plant was providing electricity, natural gas was made available, and a winery and a panel factory were established.

In 1905, a devastating fire destroyed a great portion of the business district. The merchants promptly rebuilt, and E. J. Bailey became one of the largest building contractors in western New York. Trolley service began in 1909 with the opening of the Buffalo and Lake Erie Trolley. Later, as modes off transportation changed and manufacturing went to light industry, Brocton's character changed. Today, it is a bedroom community, with a couple of industries, several businesses, churches, and a post office.

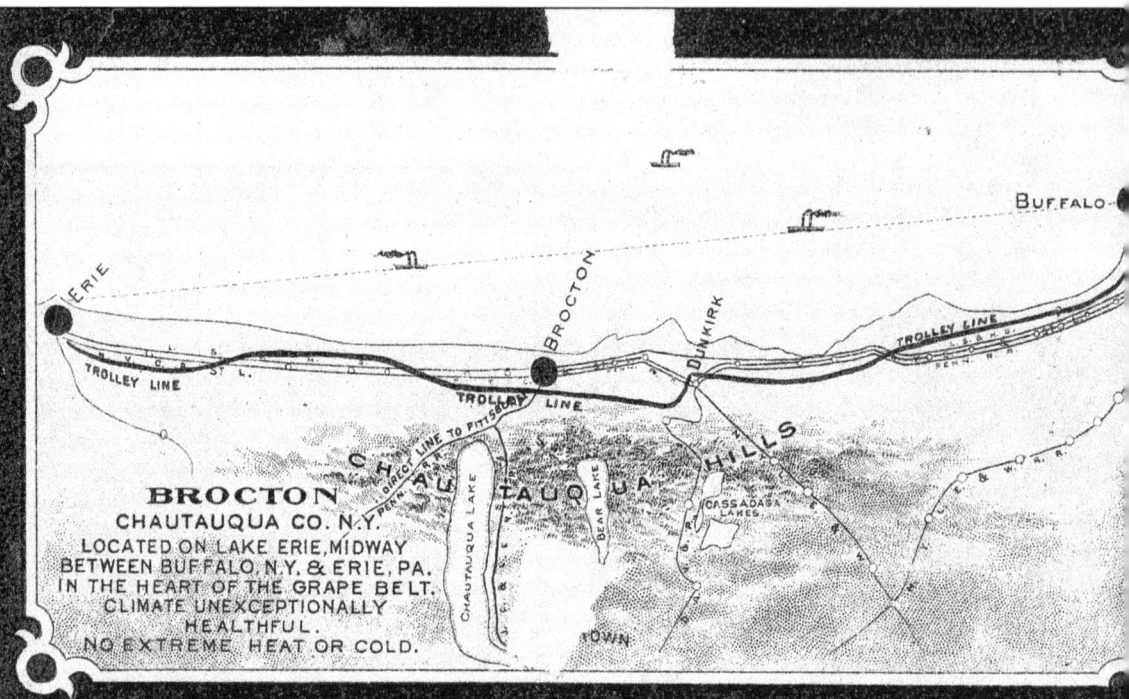

This is the back of an early printed envelope depicting the location of the village of Brocton in relationship to Chautauqua County.

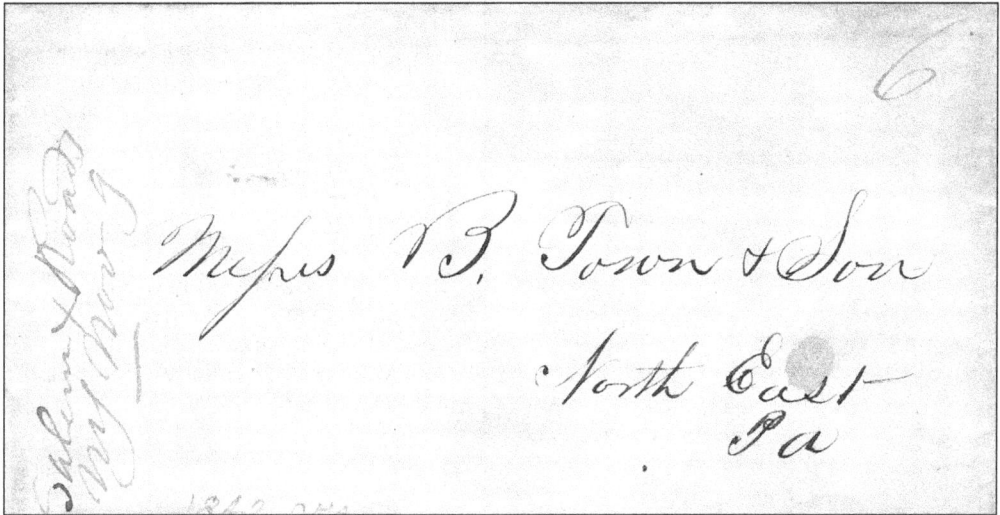

The early letters that were mailed from post offices did not use stamps. This stampless letter was mailed from Salem Cross Roads on November 9, 1842. The sender, a Mr. Morrison, was requesting a cask of salts from this store owner.

The earliest name for the village of Brocton was called Salem or Salem Cross Roads. This covered wagon drawn by two horses and pulling cattle was exhibited in the Portland Centennial in 1913. This photograph was taken going west on Main Street in the village.

In the early days of Salem, socials were very important for the residents to find out the latest news. It was very important for the residents to find out and participate in the political process. This is an invitation to attend an American Oyster Supper on December 1, 1854, at the American Hotel in Salem. The supper celebrated the victory of the American party in the 33rd Congressional District of New York State. On the committee was Z. L. Goodsell, J. Furman, D. G. Goodrich, W. I. Minton, R. D. Fuller, A. Bowdish, and R. C. Blood.

The American Hotel was the center of entertaining in early Salem Cross Roads. Here is a lovely invitation to attend an independence ball on July 4, 1853. The J. Tomkin's Band provided the music. Note the honorary managers were from Centerville in Portland, Milford in Lamberton, and Salem. The honorary managers were Harve Northup, Lemuel Webster, John Crocker, L. C. Blood, Martin Driggs, William J. Sprague, Theodore S. Moss, A. W. Baker, M. W. Richardson, Henry Baker, Mark Haight, A. J. Merrick, and Jonas Martin.

This is another invitation to celebrate the glorious fourth. Note the humor in the writing of notice. "Patriots, Attend! Relieving in a strict observance of the Glorious Fourth and the Almanac makers having run Independence Day and the Fifth close together, we propose to usher in our National Anniversary by a Social Dance commencing on the eve of the 3rd of July at the Exchange Hotel in Salem." It certainly sounds like the managers of this dance sure wanted a good party. They were L. Ogden, William Wigden, P. Martin and E. S. Matthews.

Early settlers of the town celebrated Thanksgiving differently than people in the 21st century do. This is a lovely invitation for a man and his lady to attend a Thanksgiving festival on Thursday, November 29, 1855. It was held at the American Hotel at Salem Cross Roads. Again, Tomkin's Full Band provided the music. Note that the tickets cost a very high price of $2.

## Christmas Oyster Supper.

You are Respectfully Invited to Attend an Oyster Supper at the

### Hotel of D. K. Kelley,

In Salem X Roads, Friday Eve., Dec. 24, at 6 o'clock, P. M.

COMMITTEE,

| | | | |
|---|---|---|---|
| J. A. HALL, | J. H. MINTON, | T. S. MOSS, | C. KEYS, |
| WM. SPRAGUE, | L. H. DeWOLF, | R. OGDEN, | HENRY BAKER. |
| D. G. GOODRICH, | JAMES LOWELL, | D. CLEMENTS, | A. W. BAKER. |

Christmas in early Salem Cross Roads was celebrated with friends. The recipient of this invitation was invited to attend a Christmas Oyster Supper at the hotel of D. K. Kelley in Salem Cross Roads on Christmas Eve at 6:00 p.m. Kelley was one of the early owner's of the American Hotel.

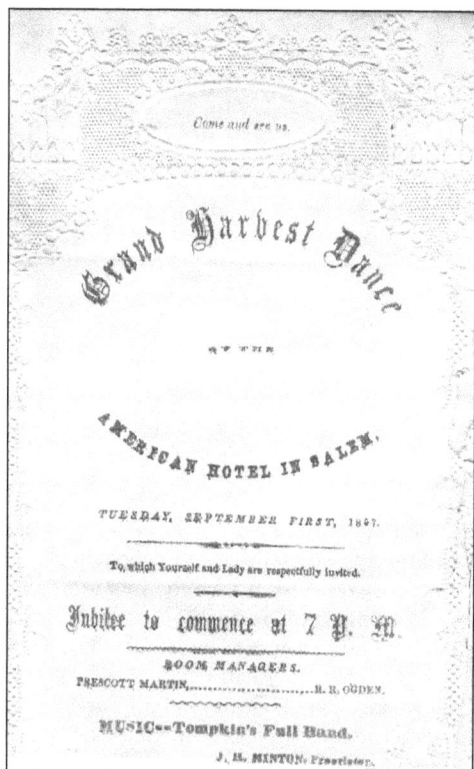

A Grand Harvest Dance was held on September 1, 1857. This Jubilee started at 7:00 p.m. and was held at the American Hotel. J. H. Minton was the proprietor. The music was provided by Tomkin's Full Band. It is important to note that there was a grand harvest that year. Farmers and merchants were very happy with the prosperous year. Furthermore this was the last year that the village was called Salem. One might speculate that the name change was discussed at this social function held at Minton's hotel. Could it possibly be Mr. Brockway was also in attendance? Seven days after this dance, the village name was changed from Salem to Brocton.

# A SOCIAL DANCE.

WILL BE HELD AT

## AMERICAN HOTEL, BROCTON,

Wednesday Evening, Jan. 13th, 1858.

### MANAGERS.

ROBERT SMITH, | MICHAEL MAHONEY,
JOHN BARRY, | MARTIN MAHER.

*Room Manager*—JOHN BARRY.

*MUSIC.....................DUNKIRK COTILLION BAND.*

By 1858, Salem Cross Roads had changed its name to Brocton. This invitation is for a social dance to be held at the American Hotel in Brocton on Wednesday, January 13, 1858. Music was provided by the Dunkirk Cotillion Band. Entertainment was very important during the entire week. This was especially true during the long winter.

THAT OYSTER SUPPER
OF HUNT'S,
WILL COME OFF AT
The Exchange, Brocton,
TUESDAY EVENING, MARCH 1st, 1859, AT 6 O'CLOCK P. M.

WILL YOU COME?

MUSIC FURNISHED BY THE COMPANY,
Bill - - - - - - $1.00.

In 1859, social functions continued to be popular during the middle part of the week. Here is a ticket to That Oyster Supper of Hunt's, which was held on March 1, 1859, at the Exchange Hotel in Brocton. Music was furnished by the company.

Map of BROCTON. *Scale 40 Rods to the Inch.*

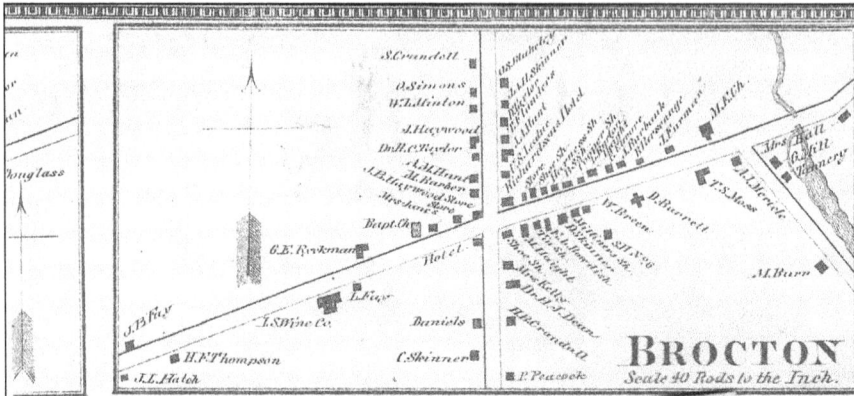

**BROCTON BUSINESS DIRECTORY.**

ne Company...Manufacturers of Native Grape
arkling Catawba Champagne and Brandies.
ysician and Surgeon.
n...Proprietor and Keeper of American Hotel.
vood...Dealers in Dry Goods, Groceries, Hard-
ckery, Boots & Shoes, Ready-made Clothing,
dicines, Yankee Notions, &c. Cash paid for
of Produce.
..Dealers in Dry Goods, Groceries, Crockery,
l Shoes, Ready-made Clothing, Drugs, Medi-
ukee Notions, &c. Cash paid for all kinds of

G. B. Carpenter...Harness Maker.
Wm. Breen...Blacksmith.
H. B. Crandall...Wagon Maker.
O. S. Blakeley...Sewing Machine Agent.
J. J. Miller...Carpenter and Joiner.
L. Lathrop...Painter.
G. Lorling...Manufacturer of Wine.
J. H. Webster...Mason.
O. L. Ogden...Manufacturer of House Furniture.
Wm. C. Burr...Farm of 140, on Lot 11, for Sale.

By 1863, as this map and directory show, Brocton was a bustling village. There was a large array of different shops and services such as dry goods, wine, house furniture, carpenters, a sewing machine agent, a blacksmith, harness and wagon makers, and hotel proprietors.

USE "MINERS" SOAP!

*Brocton, N. Y.*_____188

M_____

Bought of A. BLOOD,

DEALER IN

CHOICE FAMILY GROCERIES.

THIS SOAP CONTAINS NO STARCH

This shows the back of a Victorian trade card advertising soap found at Augusta Blood's General Store in Brocton. Blood was born in Sweden and came to this country with his parents. When he four years old he was adopted by Asa Blood of Portland. He was very intellectual and became a teacher in Brocton and in Illinois. His wife, Hattie LeDue, was also from Portland. He enlisted in the 112th New York Volunteer Infantry and served during the Civil War. After the war he became a businessman, postmaster, and supervisor of Portland. He died in Brocton, and a street is named in his honor.

By the late 1880s, another place to socialize was established. This invitation is for a grand ball given by the Old Folks of Portland at the Opera House in Brocton on Friday, March 22, 1887. Johnson Full Orchestra of Jamestown provided the music. The dance, including supper, was $1.50. No objectionable persons were admitted. There were 32 dances, with dinner after the 16th dance. The Opera House was located on what is now Highland Avenue, just south of Main Street.

GRAND BALL,

Given by

The Old Folks of Portland,

At Brocton, in Opera Hall,

Friday Eve., Mar. 22nd, 1889.

Yourself and Ladies are Cordially

Invited to Attend

Johnsons Full Orchestra of Jamestown, N. Y.

Bill, with Supper, $1.50.

No objectionable persons will be admitted.

✳ BENEFIT ∶ DANCE ! ✳

Yourself and Ladies are Cordially Invited to Attend a Benefit Hop at the

Opera House, Brocton, N. Y.,

FRIDAY EVE., MAY 16, 1890.

MUSIC BY SEYMOUR'S ORCHESTRA.

DANCE BILL SEVENTY-FIVE CENTS.

Floor Managers—Ora Tucker, J. A. LaDue, Elmer Brainard, Mike Hehir.

Invitation Committee—Vernon Mathews, G. I. Rosseter.

If people were in need, early residents always did things to help. This is an invitation to a benefit dance held at the Opera House on Friday evening May 16, 1890. Ora Tucker, J. A. LaDue, Elmer Brainard, and G. I. Rosseter were the floor managers. The invitation committee members were Vernou Mathews and G. I. Rosseter. Music was provided by Seymour's Orchestra. Cost for the dance bill was 75¢.

35

# Sons of Veterans' Dance.

Yourself and Ladies are Cordially Invited to Attend a Social Hop
to be given in the

## OPERA HOUSE,

## Brocton, Friday Evening, Sept. 22, 1893.

### MUSIC, SEYMOUR'S ORCHESTRA.

COMMITTEE--VERNON MATHEWS, J. W. BULLOCK, A. S. SMITH.

Vernon Mathews, J. W. Bullock, and A. S. Smith were the committee that sponsored a social hop held at the Opera House on September 22, 1893. Music was provided by Seymour's Orchestra.

ST. STEPHEN HOTEL, BROCTON, N. Y.

This *c.* 1912 postcard is of the St. Stephens Hotel that held so very many grand socials, dances, and celebrations throughout the history of the town. The former names of this hotel were the American Hotel and the Exchange Hotel. There were many owners and alterations to this beautiful building. One of the former owners, Mr. Cray, purchased a beautiful ornate mahogany bar in South Dayton that was originally from the Columbian Exposition in 1893. Cray transported the bar back to the St. Stephens Hotel by horse and wagon. Also in the hotel in the men's room were two huge Victorian urinals that stood over four feet high. The hotel is still in business.

Here is an advertisement card for the village of Brocton from about 1910. It lists the industries, grape shippers, business owners, churches, school, library, and railroads. There are statements of "local natural gas unlimited" and more industries wanted in the village. A very interesting notation states "8,000 cars of grapes shipped per annum" at a value of $2 million.

This canceled check was drawn on an account from the State Bank of Brocton. It was written on March 23, 1899, by L. H. Burton and made payable to C. A. Rood for $7.54, changed to $7.56. The original officers of the bank were president R. A. Hall, vice president H. J. Dean, and cashier L. D. Sullivan. The Burtons were farmers in town, and Rood was a merchant.

In 1906, Brocton's East Main Street was very full with businesses as this postcard shows. E. G. Edmunds Hardware was one of the more important stores at that time. Edmunds was a dealer in hardware, stoves and ranges, paints, oils, and so on.

MAIN STREET LOOKING WEST - BROCTON. NEW YORK.

This 1907 postcard shows Main Street looking west in the village of Brocton. Several of the buildings are still standing and in use. The one business that stands out here is the billiard hall across the street from the St. Stephens Hotel.

Grocery stores were very well stocked as this 1910 postcard shows. W. H. Manton and his son owned this market and sent this card out to customers inviting them to attend the store's annual 10 percent discount sale, which started on Thursday, February 24, and ended on March 5, 1910. The sale included everything in the store. Manton is photographed in his store along with his pet dog.

Charles Osgood is standing in front of his store Osgood and Fox Furniture, co-owned by William Fox. As this 1909 real-photo postcard shows, the store sold fine furniture. Osgood also had an undertaker business. He was always dressed very professionally.

The village of Brocton was extremely fortunate to have progressive leadership in its early days. By the early 1900s, the village had all modern utilities. The public water supply source was from a reservoir off Burr Road southeast in the hills of Portland. This is a 1908 postcard with a view of the reservoir.

Another modern utility was the village-owned Power House that generated its own electricity for the businesses and residents. Critics of the municipal-owned electric said it would loose money. However the first year showed $150 profit. This proved to be a great asset to the businesses and industries of the village. This postcard shows a picture the Power House. It was located on what is now Highland Avenue south of the railroad tracts.

Ahira Hall Memorial Library, Brocton, N. Y.          Ralph H. Hall, Its Donor.

In 1905, Ralph H. Hall donated a building for a library that would service and be owned by the town on land that was donated by G. Rykeman. The library donation had one stipulation: If the building ceased to be used as a library, the building was to be given back to the family. The beautiful building was erected and housed two reading rooms and a book storage room. It had fancy oak woodwork and two lovely fireplaces. In modern times, the town offices were in the basement for over 30 years until a new town office building was erected in 1998. This 1910 postcard depicts the Ahira Hall Memorial Library with a photograph of its donor, Ralph H. Hall. The library is still in use.

**ROSSITER PHARMACY**
THE PRESCRIPTION DRUG STORE
Main Street          •          Brocton, New York

L. S. Rossiter                              Phone SY 2-3551

DATE

Today's Prescription – Your Biggest Health Value

1892     Geo l Rossiter  to   1896

One of the early stores in the village, Rossiter Pharmacy was a family business for many years. In began in 1892 as the George Rossiter Company, and then it was known as Peoples Store Dry Goods and Millenary from 1896 until 1910. In 1902, Rossiter added the name Rossiter Drug Company until 1914. Finally the business became Rossiter Pharmacy from 1925 until 1965. One could always go into the pharmacy, sit at the counter, and sip a great soda fountain drink. This building was located on East Main Street across from the Methodist Church.

Gimmick advertising was as important to businesses in the early days as it is today. Mr. Manton gave out these wonderful calendar advertisements with sewing needles in 1908. It was made by the London Needle Company of New York.

This is the backside of the needles advertisement and calendar. The best part on this side of the advertisement is the little poem which reads "Remember Miss or Madam fair, There's one who will not brook, An angry word or look from you—Do not cross the cook. Go where she bids you buy the food, Don't get into a fuss, When she insists—she knows the best—That you shall buy from us."

| OSBRON W. BENNETT | ISSUED TO |
| Chautauqua Lake ICE | |
| PORTLAND, N. Y. - 1,000 Lbs. - PHONE 1782 | NO. 3 DATE July 24 19 36 |

Residents needed ice to keep their perishables cold that they purchased at the local grocery stores. Osbron W. Bennett operated the Chautauqua Lake Ice Company in the 1930s. This is a prepaid card issued to Monty Burton of Brocton on July 24, 1936. When Burton picked up his ice blocks, Bennett punched each weight size that was taken.

E. J. Bailey, a building contractor from the village of Brocton, was considered one of the best builders in western New York. Bailey's salesroom and yards were up by the Pennsylvania Railroad track on South Street (now Highland Avenue). After a devastating fire in the business district of the village that destroyed some buildings, Bailey built a new store and office building on the northeast side of Main Street at the four corners. This building was known as the Bailey Building and housed stores and offices. In modern years (1930 through the 1990s), the post office was located on the Lake Avenue side of the building. The basement housed Bert Medd Wallpaper and Paint. Attorney's offices and the town court were located on the second floor.

# E. J. BAILEY
## BUILDING CONTRACTOR
### DEALER IN LUMBER, LATH, HARDWARE AND BUILDING SUPPLIES OF ALL KINDS

YARDS AND SALES ROOM AT
SOUTH STREET, PENN. RAILROAD

BROCTON, N. Y.,  May 19 1923

SOLD TO     Montie Burton,

TERMS                      City

| | | | | |
|---|---|---|---|---|
| 7 tile | @ $1.50 | | $10. | 50 |

*Received Payment 6/5/23*
*E J Bailey*

E. J. Bailey not only was a building contractor but also a "dealer in lumber, lath, hardware, and building supplies of all kinds." This is a 1923 paid receipt in the amount of $10.50 for seven tiles sold to Monty Burton.

Bailey did not only build businesses, he constructed some grand and glorious homes. This is a postcard looking north on Highland Avenue in the village. The first house pictured on left was the home that Bailey built for himself. The interior of the home is as beautiful as the exterior. The main living area had beautifully decorated tin panels of grapes on the walls along with very ornate oak cabinetry and woodwork. In modern times, the home has become the Morse Funeral Home. Many of the original elements still remain.

44

The village of Brocton had a very active citizen's band. They provided music in the area, traveled, and also performed at funerals. The original members were Thomas Capwell, Carl Risley, John Love, Frank Mosher, E. S. Moss, T. C. Moss, Ranson Haight, William Miles Gust Timell, and A. B. Cook as instructor. This is a 1906 photograph of the band before one of their performances.

Crandall's Hardware Store was located on the south side of West Main Street next to the St. Stephens Hotel. Moss Hall owned the building. Two men are standing in the doorway of this business. The horse and wagon are waiting for the purchased supplies.

Early water bills covered six-month periods. C. W. Burton paid this water bill at the State Bank of Brocton on November 15, 1901. There evidently were no late charges applied as it was paid five days after the due date. The total as $5.76, which included domestic use, plain bibby for $2, water closet for $1, carriage for 50¢, two horses for $1.13, and three cows for $1.13.

BROCKTON, N. Y.

H*ello* HiRAM:-

i was chused to give you a invite to the doins at josh harden's Two-Step factory Thespain haul,

**Saturday Nite, March 20th**

**YOU'LL** *Have* **to HURRY.** Hi and git your chorse did up early fer the doins starts at 8:30 and won't be over til midnight neither.

Harden lows he'll let we'ns jig fer the same old price he allus does so git your togs in trim and send fer mandy and i reckon we'll have the swellest time cause dudes with city close or biled shirts not be aloud to dance till after ten o'clock.

## *Grand* **Concert**

by the WINDJAMMERS BAND at 8:30

REWARD fer the best togged feller and gal a grand prize will be given. fair judges by experts.

## GRAND PRIZE

fer the best hop waltzer.

HINTS: Gentlemen wear large straw or old felt hats, jumpers and overalls, long legged boots; any kind of old costume.

Whiskers and wigs if you wish.

Ladies wear large aprons or old style dresses. For hats any old summer hat trimmed for the occasion, or if you prefer, sunbonnets.

P. S.—No mask will be permitted.

This early-1900s notice invites those to attend "the doins at josh harden's Two-Step factory Thespain haul, Saturday Nite, March 20th . . . 8:30 . . . til midnight . . . Grand Concert by the Windjammers Band at 8:30." There also was a grand prize for the best hop waltzer. Attendees had to dress in old time clothes but without masks. The Thespian Hall was on East Main Street on the second floor of the Brocton State Bank Building.

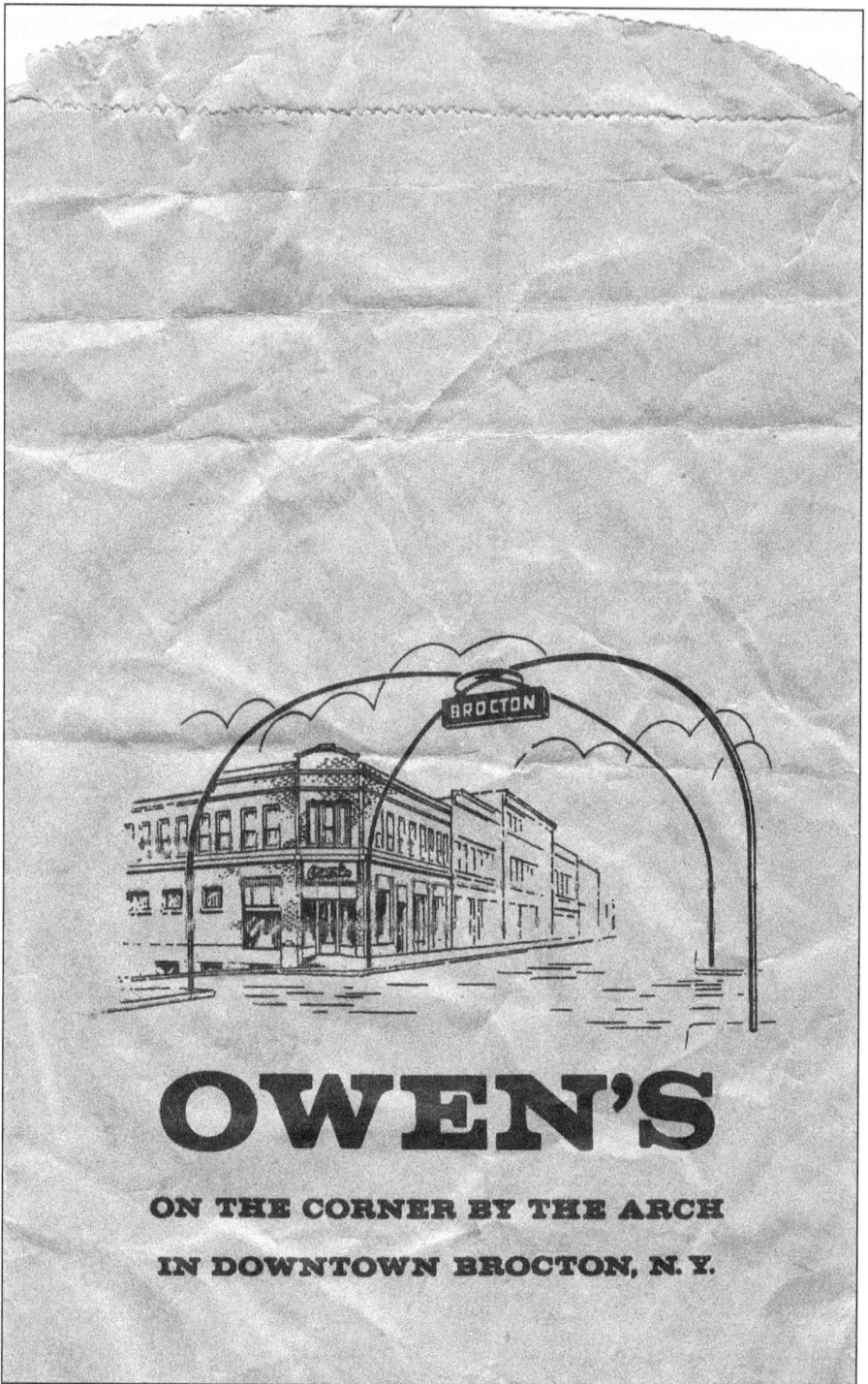

OWEN'S

ON THE CORNER BY THE ARCH

IN DOWNTOWN BROCTON, N.Y.

Generations of residents would shop at Owen's to buy a card, newspaper, paint, or other goods. Bob and Marge Owens were the owners. Florabell Graham and Angie Cutrona were the salesclerks. If one bought something from Bob Owen, he would say, "Do you want that in a poke?" Bright memories come from a paper bag.

Band concerts were always wonderful entertainment. Everyone had a chance to get out and hear good music as well as converse with people. This flyer for a band concert announces that the program would be tonight. Although the date is not known, it is probably from the early 1900s, and looks like it would be an enjoyable evening.

**TO-NIGHT! ✦ TO-NIGHT!**

**Band Concert.**

**Entire Change of Programme.**

PART FIRST.

| | |
|---|---|
| Love's Dream Land Waltzes, | Band |
| Overture, | Orchestra |
| Duet, | |
| Old Fashioned Church on the Hill, | Mr. and Mrs. Sullivan |
| Instrumental Solo, | |
| Drondenschen, (Franz Bendel) | Miss Aura Lowell |
| Recitation, | |
| Tim Crane's Proposal, | Miss Minnie La Due |
| Solo, | |
| Love's Golden Dream, (Lindsey) | Miss Eva Hall |
| Duet, | |
| Catherina, | Mike and Biddy |
| Solo, | |
| Love's Sorrow, | F. B. Whipple |
| Selection, | Orchestra |

PART SECOND.

Grand Minstrel Overture,

| | |
|---|---|
| Solo, | E. Mathews |
| Solo, | C. R. Barnhart |
| Solo, | F. B. Whipple |
| Duet, | |
| Lost Ship, | Messrs. Wilcox and Sullivan |
| Solo, | |
| Rockaby Baby, | Mrs. L. D. Sullivan |
| Octet, | |
| Italia, Beloved, | (From Costa's Chorus) |
| Overture, | Orchestra |
| Evening Breeze Waltzes, | Band |

**GOOD NIGHT.**

**The Columbian Lyceum,**

SATURDAY EVENING, March 10th.

COMPLIMENTS OF THE GRAPE BELT.

THE PEOPLE'S
DRY GOODS STORE,
Rossiter Block,
G. I. ROSSITER, Proprietor.

S. J. CLARK
Fire, Life and Accident
INSURANCE

G. S. OWEN
Gents' Furnishing Goods,
HATS and CAPS.
ALSO A FULL LINE OF
Boots and Shoes.

E. C. EDMUNDS.
Hardware, Tinware, Stoves
And all kinds of Farm Implements.

G. M. MATHEWS & CO.,
DRY GOODS AND GROCERIES.

PROGRAM
Music. Orchestra
Reading, Original Poem, Mrs. E. P. Harris
Duet, Mr. and Mrs. L. D. Sullivan
Music, Orchestra
Recitation, Mrs. C. F. Crandal
Instrumental Duet, Misses Moss and Reckey
Music, Orchestra
Debate: Resolved that the annexation of Canada would be detrimental to the United States.
Affirmative: F. G. Crane, C. L. Risteard, Dr. Cleveland, Chas. Barton, Wm. Ogilvie.
Negative: W. C. Willett, R. A. Hall, Geo. L. Henley, Chas. Henley, A. A. Skinner.

OSGOOD & FOX,
Furniture Dealers
AND UNDERTAKERS.

F. W. PECK,
Dry Goods, Groceries, Provisions,
BOOTS and SHOES.

C. F. CRANDALL,
DEALER IN
Shelf and Heavy Hardware, Stoves, Refrigerators,
AGRICULTURAL IMPLEMENTS'
3 STANDARD BOOKS FREE 3
TO SUBSCRIBERS.
See announcement in The Grape Belt.

T. B. HARLEY & SON.
Cutters and Sleighs.
Horseshoeing a Specialty.

FRANK WESTERLING,
Flour and Feed
Fuchman Building

Westfield Steam Laundry,
Laundry delivered and collected.

FLOYD FURMAN, Agt,
Laundry leaves Wednesday afternoon,
returning Friday afternoon.

The Columbia Lyceum was located on Highland Avenue. The newspaper, the *Grape Belt*, printed this program. Just like today, the newspaper sold advertisements from local merchants. The year is not stated, but presumably it is around the beginning of the 20th century. The program is important because local leaders debated whether the annexation of Canada would be detrimental to the United States.

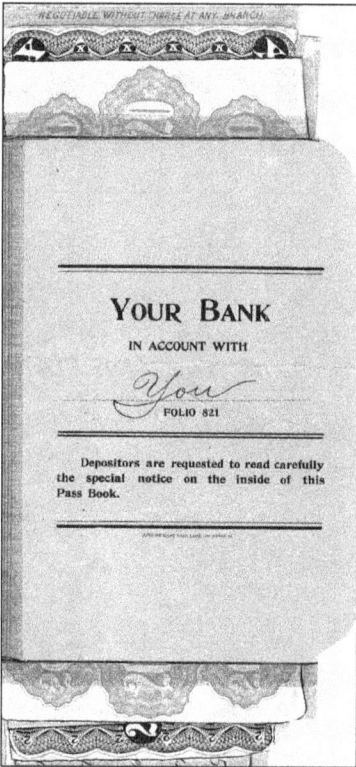

In 1906, the local bank had these colorful flyers printed that advertised a mid-winter fair in Brocton on January 16–19, 1906, under the auspices of Citizen's Hose and Citizen's Bank of Brocton. L. R. Ryckman was the president and John Campbell was the secretary of Citizen's Bank at that time.

One should not write about the history of the town of Portland without recognizing the most outstanding historian of the town. This was H. C. Taylor, who was a Civil War physician, local doctor for many years, served on the Chautauqua County Board of Supervisors, and wrote a history of the town of Portland in 1873. This book became "the Bible" for other historians due to the way it was written, presented, and researched. He loved his history and the town. This is a photograph of him with his horse and carriage.

**The Following is the Financial Condition o. this Association at the Close of Business Dec. 31, 1919. (Two Months.)**

| Disbursements | | Receipts | |
|---|---|---|---|
| Paid for supplies | 117.22 | Dues, members | 10,579.25 |
| Salaries | 30.00 | Entrance Fees | 178.25 |
| Cash on hand | 10,610.83 | Fines | .55 |
| | $10,758.05 | | $10,758.05 |

We had on this date 140 members holding shares of a matured value $95,750,00.

Brocton Building. Savings & Loan Association,

W. N. Clark, Secretary.

Brocton Building Savings and Loan was created around 1919 in Brocton. This is an advertisement stating its financial condition in 1919. Note that supplies cost far more than was paid out for salaries. The company remained for many years and disbanded around 1970.

*The DeLuxe Paint for all Surfaces*

**BURT MEDD W. P. & PAINT**
36 W. Main Street · BROCKTON, N. Y.
Phone 2083

Bert Medd opened and operated a wallpaper and paint store at 36 West Main Street in Brocton. He later moved his business into the basement of Bob Owens's building. Medd was one of the few local veterans of the Spanish American War. He was also an accomplished musician and played organ for many years in the Salem Lutheran Church in Brocton.

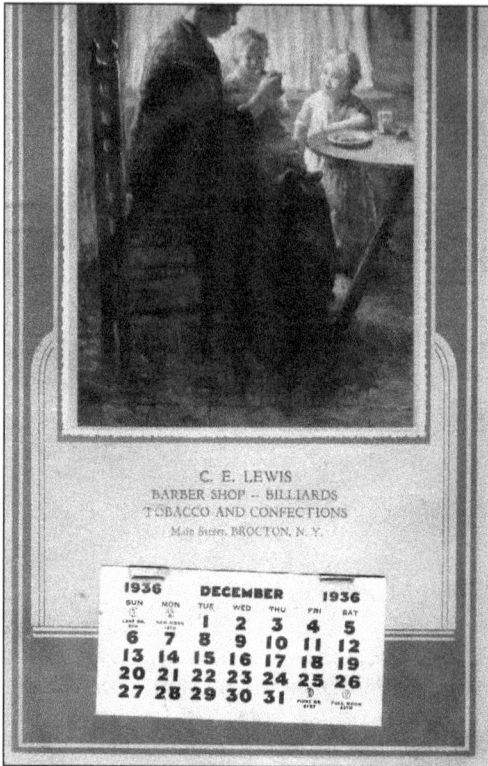

C. E. Lewis owned and operated a general store on Main Street in Brocton. There, one could get a haircut, purchase cigars and candy, and then play some billiards. This is a 1936 advertising calendar from his business.

C. E. LEWIS
BARBER SHOP ~ BILLIARDS
TOBACCO AND CONFECTIONS
Main Street, BROCTON, N. Y.

| 1936 | | DECEMBER | | | 1936 | |
|---|---|---|---|---|---|---|
| SUN | MON | TUE | WED | THU | FRI | SAT |
| | | 1 | 2 | 3 | 4 | 5 |
| 6 | 7 | 8 | 9 | 10 | 11 | 12 |
| 13 | 14 | 15 | 16 | 17 | 18 | 19 |
| 20 | 21 | 22 | 23 | 24 | 25 | 26 |
| 27 | 28 | 29 | 30 | 31 | | |

ARCH PARK
CREATED BY THE BROCTON MAIN STREET REVITALIZATION COMMITTEE
DAVID E. TRAVIS, CHAIRMAN     DR. FRANKLIN B. KROHN, VICE CHAIRMAN
DAN SCHRANTZ, VICE CHAIRMAN     INEZ C. KROHN, SECRETARY
DEDICATED MAY 29, 1999

In 1999, the Brocton Revitalization Committee held a fund-raiser selling memorial bricks to create the Brocton Arch Park. This is the plaque that is erected near the Brocton Arch giving its information.

# Four

# VINEYARD

When the Pennsylvania Railroad came to the Brocton station, the area north of Main Street became busy and a post office was needed. On March 11, 1898, a post office was established and the station was named Grapes. This was an appropriate choice because this was in the middle of Chautauqua County's grape belt and was surrounded by vineyards. Charles Kinney was appointed postmaster. No one knows what the reason was, but on April 7, 1898, the name was changed to Vineyard. This post office was closed September 15, 1931.

Vineyard was a hub of activity, and businesses and services were established. There were two railroad stations, a post office, businesses that utilized the railway system for transport were erected close to the tracks, and a grand hotel was built to accommodate the travelers and railroad employees. The potential for fire was very much on people's minds even before the official naming of Vineyard. On June 10, 1896, Brocton Hose Company No. 1 was organized at the home of Charles Kinney. Seven men were present at that meeting and every one of them was elected to an office. Charles Kinney and William Ogilvie became the foreman and assistant foreman, respectfully. Edward Mathews was elected secretary and Benjamin Cochrane became the treasurer. Elected trustees were T. G. Connors, A. J. Billings, and W. J. Balcom. At their second meeting on June 16, 1896, the company introduced their used hand carriage that they purchased in Jamestown for $50, which the village reimbursed them for. The first "Hose House" for the carriage was on the south side of Kinney Street owned by Jonas Martin. This company eventually merged with the uptown fire company to become the Brocton Fire Department. Eventually another smaller hotel opened. After the railroad stopped servicing the area, Vineyard became a quiet area with just the hotels and feed mill in operation. Presently a hotel and scrap and auto salvage businesses are operating in the area.

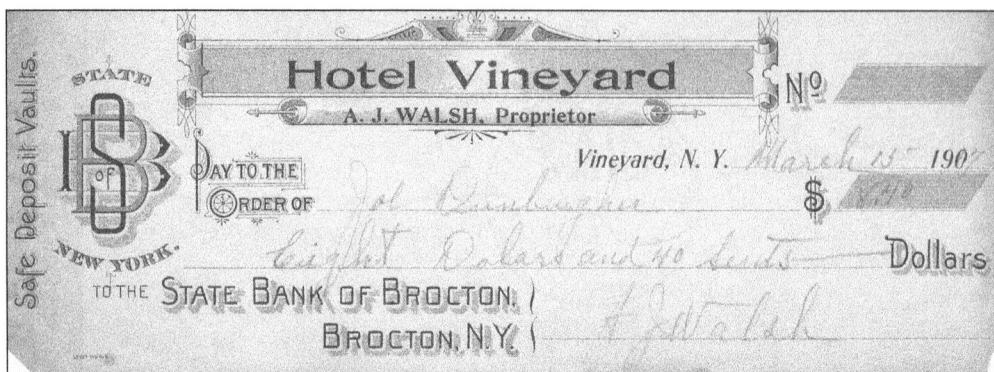

Newly Furnished      Both 'Phones      Near Depots

## HOTEL VINEYARD

A. J. WALSH, Prop.

BROCTON,  -  -  NEW YORK

Rates $1.50 Per Day

The Hotel Vineyard became the hub of activity. It was owned and operated by A. J. Walsh. The magnificent three-story hotel had wrap-around porches on two floors. The first floor had the bar, dining room, and post office. The tin ceiling in the dining room was adorned with hand-painted flowers. On Walsh's business card, he states the hotel is newly furnished with "both" phones, near depots, and the rates were $1.50 per day. Two generations of the Walsh family owned the hotel. The hotel closed in the 1960s.

In 1872, 36,000 passengers and 190,000 lbs. of freight were transferred at this station.

The Pennsylvania Railroad was also called Vineyard the Brocton Junction because it was the last stop before the trains went over the hills toward Pennsylvania. This image from an envelope shows some railroad workers relaxing next to the Pennsylvania Railroad Depot. The sign reads "Brocton Junction Forty Five Minutes from Chautauqua on Chautauqua Lake." Written on the back of this postcard is L. S. M. S. George Carpenter, A. Balcomb, L. S. M. S. Carpenter, L.S and M.S. Carpenter, Gary Cone (agent), Homer Francis, Major Tucker (in overalls), Jake Boyland, Gene Furman, and Will Dorn. The note below the image states that in 1872, 36,000 passengers and 190,000 pounds of freight were transferred at this station.

54

William H. Allen owned and operated a carriage service from the Lake Shore and Michigan Southern Railway and Pennsylvania Railroad depots in Vineyard. His carriage was highly decorated. He transported passengers from Vineyard uptown to the village of Brocton in style. This photograph shows Allen waiting for passengers in front of the Pennsylvania Railroad Depot. One of his early advertisements reads, "You get the very best of Livery service if you see W. H. Allen. If you wish to meet the train, call up Bell 12 or Local 62, and the bus will call for you. If you wish to go driving let us know and we will have a rig ready for you. Baggage transferred."

PENNSYLVANIA R. R. STATION - BROCTON. NEW YORK.

This postmarked 1907 Vineyard postcard shows the east side of Vineyard. The building in the foreground is the Pennsylvania Railroad Station. The next building is the Brocton Wine and Distilling Company. The building with the awning was the small hotel later to be known as Densmore's. Today it is the Nickel Plate Depot Restaurant.

This is an unused coupon for half fare aboard the New York Central Railroad from Brocton. The New York Central Railroad was originally the Buffalo and Erie Railroad, which changed its name to Lake Shore and Michigan Southern Railway, and then finally it became the New York Central Railroad.

Henry Roff from Portland purchased 30 shares of a very young Buffalo and Erie Railroad Company on November 8, 1831. His down payment was $2 a share and was ordered to pay $48 on each share in installments when required to by the board of directors of the company. The shares transaction was a very early issue No. 7.

Major businesses were located in Vineyard that used the railroad for shipping out their goods. Crandall Panel Company made veneer and grape baskets, and the company's building sat along side the tracks for easy loading. A subsidiary of this company was the Vineyard Basket Company, which employed 40 men and was also housed in the building. They produced 8,000 baskets every week. This is a 1912 real-photo postcard of the modern, three-story building for the business that employed both young and old. The recipient of this card was A. H. Walker of Silver Creek. Jay Crandall, owner of the business, wrote that they "got a new Clerk. she is a dandy, first two days."

This is a photograph of the laborers at the Crandall Panel Factory taken in the early 1900s. Identified here are Hosea Crandall (in doorway), Vern Mathews (sitting), Bert Rose, Duane Gardiner (standing), Dick Bloomfield, Tom Gregory, Ed Rose, ? Connor, Ed Spencer, Cub Swanson, Gene Furman, Washington Bloomfield, Stanley Barber (in window), Linus Anderson, Kudglan, James Throne, Jack Dunn, ? Connor, ? Mechan, Ed Carey, Major Tucker, Will Bremer (in door), Ed Berg, boy (possibly a Gregory), and little Tom Gregory.

This is a 1925 calendar given out by Vernon Mathews, who was a dealer in flour, feed, and grain. A. A. Fay owned this mill for two years before selling it to Mathews, a former Crandall Panel Company employee. Mathews named the business Brocton Mills. He manufactured 25 barrels of flour and feed daily. It was a very large local business that shipped out large amounts of flour and feed. The business was later sold to Lee Blodgett, and finally closed in the early 1970s.

LAKE SHORE R. R. STATION - BROCTON, NEW YORK.

Lake Shore Railroad also had a station at Vineyard. This is a postcard postmarked in 1906 that shows the Lake Shore Railroad Station at Brocton.

# Five

# SUMMER COMMUNITIES

The northern boundary of Portland abuts the Lake Erie shoreline. Since the mid-1870s, summer cottages and lakefront homes have sprung up along the coastline. There are three major lakefront communities that were established since that time that have remained busy summer areas.

Van Buren Point is the earliest of these summer resorts. This private association was laid out in 1877 by D. Fairbanks. Owners paid taxes to the town but the roads were maintained by the association rather than the town. The Portland-Pomfret town line crossed the eastern portion of Van Buren Point at an angle, placing a small portion of the point into Pomfret Township. In 1836, a Van Buren Company purchased 300 acres at Van Buren Harbor, adjoining the point. This acreage was laid out in building lots. Rumors spread that Van Buren Harbor was to be a western terminal of the New York and Erie Railroad instead of Dunkirk. One Canadian purchased 24 lots to build businesses four stories high. Some people sold their homes in this area at inflated prices. Eli T. Foote, an important businessman and politician from Jamestown, wrote to an attorney, J. H. Hubbard on February 17, 1836, to say that the price for lots at Van Buren Harbor had been puffed. Shares of stock in Van Buren Harbor sold for nearly $3,000 each. He felt that it was a better deal to buy in Portland Harbor, a few miles west of Van Buren Harbor, where lots were only $300–$400. Van Buren Harbor boomed until 1851 when the railroad went to Dunkirk.

Greencrest adjoins Van Buren Point to the west. This also was a private summer community. The community runs along the lakefront with four connecting roads to Route 5. They dissolved the association in modern times, and it now is a residential area of the town.

Farther west along Route 5, there are two small summer resort areas. Green Hills on the Lake has a small grouping of summer and year around homes. Portland Bay, a couple of miles farther west, was created in the 1930s by Portland Bay Association by selling stock certificates. It is still in existence with several cottages in the area.

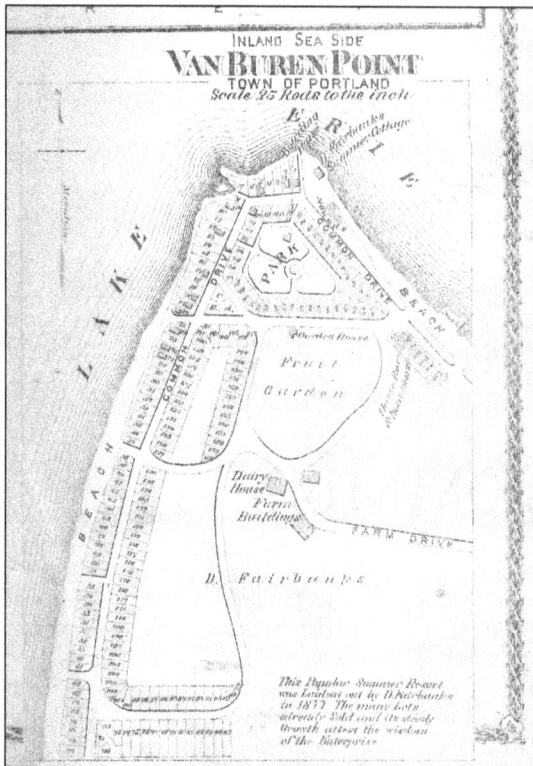

This 1881 map of Van Buren Point taken from the 1863 *Chautauqua County Atlas* shows the layout of the point. Today the cottage layout is still the same. Generations of families have owned the cottages. Many homes are being updated but still retain their Victorian flair. The area is very busy in the summer with activities for all ages of the residents. People from all over the country as well as Canada are owners.

The point has many rocks and cliffs. This postcard from about 1918 shows a great view of Pulpit Rock at Van Buren Point. There are many high cliffs along the lake. Storms have caused Lake Erie's water to erode the shoreline and wash away valuable land. In the 1990s, the association built a break wall to ward off further erosion of the shoreline.

This real-photo postcard that was postmarked in 1909 is of Hull's Beach in Portland, which was west of Van Buren Point. The high bank that one had to go down to get to the beach is visible. The swimming and sand were worth the climb. In the background, one can also see Pulpit Rock at Van Buren Point.

Just east of the mouth of Slippery Rock Creek was known as Wenborne Cliffs. The Wenborne's were prominent citizens in town. Their lovely craftsman home is shown in this postcard. Many swimmers would reach the beach area at the mouth of the creek. Erosion has washed away much of these cliffs.

Bathing at Corells Beach, near Brocton, N. Y.

Corell's Beach is at the end of Pecor Street in Portland. There is a huge rock a short distance out from the shore. It is a popular spot for swimmers to sunbathe. This beach was easy to access with no cliffs, therefore it was a very popular spot for local and summer visitors to swim and enjoy the wonderful summer climate. This postcard shows the many swimmers.

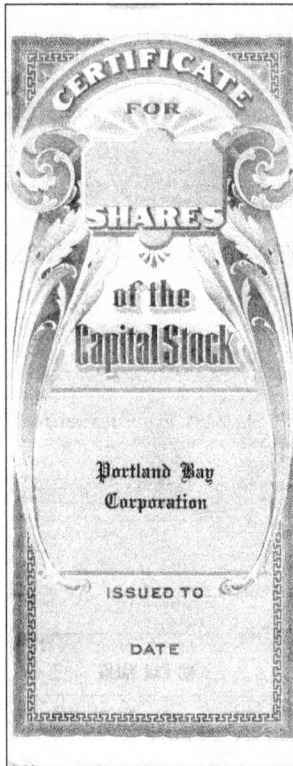

Farther west along the lake is a private summer community called Portland Bay Corporation. Shares of stock were sold for ownership. Lovely summer cottages were built for the owners to enjoy the summer months at Lake Erie. This is a stock certificate for 20 shares in Portland Bay. It was dated 1930. This private community is still in existence.

# Six

# THOMAS LAKE HARRIS

The Brotherhood of New Life was established in 1867 by Rev. Thomas Lake Harris. The community consisted of nearly 2,000 acres of farmland mainly along the lakefront. Portland was chosen for Harris Community because of the great climate for growing grapes. Salem-on-Erie was chosen by Harris as his town's name. Harris's personality was very powerful with a great power of persuasion. He recruited members of the community mainly from European and Japanese nobility. One prominent member was Lady Oliphant and her son, Laurence. Laurence Oliphant was a member of British Parliament and gave up his seat to come to the Harris Community in Portland. He became Harris's right-hand man. When converts moved to the community, all their worldly possessions were turned over to Harris. Men, women, and children lived in separate areas. The members moved from place to place on the premises for their sake of employment. They did menial work similar to what would be found on a large farm. They operated a nursery called Chautauqua County Greenhouse and Nurseries. The company name for wine made on the farm was called Lake Erie and Missouri River Wine Company. Selling wine was for "medicinal purposes only." The community also had a hotel and restaurant in their village. The children were Harris's servants. Their duties included yard work, household cleaning, and moving furniture at Harris's home, Vine Cliff. While the residents were working, Harris lived in splendor in his beautiful home. He wrote books on his theories and continued to recruit new members to his community. The community members were considered Socialists because they believed that the practical fulfillment of the Gospel was in what they termed "Divine Natural Society."

In 1875, Harris had a vision that a new community was needed in California and purchased a large tract of land in Santa Rosa. Members then left for the new community when their work was finished in Portland. Some members remained in Portland. Oliphant did not go with Harris. He and his wife went to Syria and started his own community and he sued Harris for the return of his Portland property. The courts gave him 900 acres. The remaining acres of the community were eventually sold. This officially ended the Harris Community's domain in Portland.

The map contains numerous labels including: F. R. (river/lake area), Vine Cliff, Wine Cellar, Brotherhood of the New Life, DIST, ROAD, BROCKTON P.O., PORTLAND P.O., SCHOOL, and various property owner names with acreages (J. Warner 84a, W. Fitch 20a, Mrs. N. Fitch 19a, H. Skinner, C. Rossiter 55a, J. Murphy, H. Co., Tillwe..., Peterson, P. Berg 200a, E. Gabridse 20a, ..on 46a, C. Barke 30a, Kelly Brother, New Life, C. W. Burton, 15, I. Haight No 9 Heirs 135a, C. Burton 30a, D. Cassady 36a, Belman B, J. Clavin 22a, S. Burton 40a, G. D. Tuttle 20a, Mrs. Elmore 25a, A. J. Monroe, H. B. Crandall 11a, 14, Brotherhood of the New Life, A. Vredenburg 20a, A. Vreden... 12a, Mass, 29a, DIST No 6, Helley Brothers 50a, C Van Gunsbrede 50a, F. Harp 20a, Springstead, J. E., Fletcher 88a, DIST No 7, E. Underhill 90a, 78a, W. Mungan 22a, R. P. Fuller H Hall, Brotherhood of the New Life, G. F. Kyckman 20a, G. F. Fyksa, G. F. Kyckman, J. Skinner, J. N. Porter 40a, W. Warner 43a, A. K. Thompson 65a, C. Co..., South, Saw Mill, Brotherhood of the New Life, I. Marsh 125a, J. L. Hutchson, H Thompson, J. Dinsmore, S. Hall 10a, Dunbar 15a, H. C. Moss, Burton 28a, R. H. Bird 7a, T. S. Holt, Saw Mill, W. Miles 50a, C. Warner 36a, Haight, L. Douglas, N. Rhodes, R. P. Fuller 33a, G. Warner, Hibbard)

The Harris Community included 2,000 acres in Portland. As seen in this map taken from the 1881 *Chautauqua County Atlas*, the domain went from the lakeshore area up to Main Street. The property's soil was of proper mixture for growing grapes. The homes and buildings were scattered among the acreage and Vine Cliff was Rev. Thomas Lake Harris's residence. It is interesting to note the wine cellar was approximately one mile south of his residence. The property was not only in the town but also a small portion in the village. The railroad depots were not included.

Vine Cliff was the home of Harris. It was a beautiful 24-room home elaborately built and decorated. It was rumored that there were secret panels in the living room. A lot of elegant entertaining was hosted by Harris in this home. The grounds were as lovely as the home. It is now a very well-maintained private residence. (Courtesy of Edward T. Kurtz Jr.)

Vine Cliff farms also had lovely barns. This photograph shows the front side of the main barn. Look at the beautiful stone foundation and decorative peak. It is now a private residence. (Courtesy of Edward T. Kurtz Jr.)

The Harris Community had to have a mill to grind grains. This was located on Wenborne Road off of Erie Road next to Slippery Rock Creek. Imagine wealthy men doing menial labor as running this mill. When this photograph was taken, the building was abandoned. Only the foundation area of this mill remains. (Courtesy of Edward T. Kurtz Jr.)

Beautiful pasture and hay fields were also abundant on the property. This modern-day photograph shows pasture and grape fields on the Vine Cliff property. The home is nestled in the wooded area on the left side of the photograph. Imagine wealthy men loading grapes onto wagons to take to the winery. (Courtesy of Edward T. Kurtz Jr.)

The wine cellar in the Harris Community was also a very important structure. It was located on the north side of what is now Peerless Street in the village of Brocton. The community produced between 15,000 and 23,000 gallons of wine a year. The members built this main arched and fireproof wine cellar of stone. It was 110 feet long and could hold 65,000 gallons of wine. At one time, this building was also used as a cattle barn. The cellar still exists. (Courtesy of Edward T. Kurtz Jr.)

Rev. Thomas Lake Harris became good friends with several local residents. G. E. Ryckman became a good friend because of their mutual love in wine making. Another astute resident was Stewart Dean Esq. Dean had a prominent law firm in New York City where he met Harris. Being very impressed with Dean, Harris offered him land in Portland to build a home if he would become the Harris's lawyer. Dean accepted and moved to the town were he built a beautiful Victorian home. He represented Harris in many lawsuits by former community members and families wanting there assets returned to them. When the community moved, the Dean family remained in Portland. This is a photograph of the Stewart Dean residence. (Courtesy of Edward T. Kurtz Jr.)

# Seven

# GRAPES

Deacon Elijah Fay moved to the town of Portland in 1811 from Southborough, Massachusetts, and settled at Salem Cross Roads, now the village of Brocton. He planted the first grape vine on his property in 1818. The vines grew profusely but the fruit was inferior quality. He tried again in 1822 with no luck, for the fruit mildewed. A few years later, Fay purchased William R. Prince of Flushing, Long Island, and roots of Isabella and Catawba. Those varieties grew with excellent production of fruit.

It took several years before the early settlers became familiar with the luscious flavor of these grapes. In 1830, Fay made the first juice using the Isabella and Catawba variety. In the meantime, other settlers purchased nursery stock from Lincoln Fay (son of Elisha brother to Elijah) and began growing their own vineyards.

Lincoln first introduced Concord grapes for juice in the 1850s. In 1851, Joseph Fay, son of Elijah, started growing Concord grapes, and in 1857, along with another early settler H. A. Burton, planted the first large planting of grapes on a quarter of an acre. This was the beginning of the grape industry in Portland.

The wine industry began in town with the creation of the Brocton Wine Cellars, which was established by Joseph B. Fay, Rufus Haywood, and G. E. Rykeman (Elijah Fay's son-in-law). Other wineries were also soon to be established.

With the trains servicing town, grape-related companies sprang up near the railroad. The shipping of grapes was made easier to reach markets. Many jobs were available and the town prospered. Most homes on the outskirts of the village had a grape vineyard up until the 1960s. Homemakers and children worked in the grapes—trimming, tying, and picking. The farmers' grapes at least paid their taxes and if they owned a large vineyard, it provided them a fairly decent yearly salary.

Automation of the grape industry came into existence. Self-driven grape harvesters could harvest grapes faster with fewer people. Double trellis grapes made it faster and easier to trim. Railroads stopped servicing the town. Welch's juice company, which contracted most of the modern day grapes for their juice, closed their plant in Brocton. There still are a large number of vineyards in town but most are now owned by large grape farmers. There also is one winery that produces award-winning wines.

# NOTICE.

**THE** undersigned take this method to inform the public generally, that they intend to keep the **PURE JUICE OF THE GRAPE** on hand, and will supply all those who wish, on reasonable terms. A liberal discount will be made to those who wish to purchase by the barrel.

**ELIJAH FAY & SONS.**

*The following Certificates have been received:*

Permit me to advertise the Churches that Deacon ELIJAH FAY & SONS, of Portland, Chautauque co., have several barrels of Wine, which is the pure juice of the grape—"the fruit of the Vine,"—uncontaminated with foreign ingredients of any kind, and unmixed with alcoholic liquors, which the Churches would do well to obtain for sacramental purposes. Br. Fay & Sons cultivate the ISABELLA GRAPE, from which the above wine was manufactured. J. L. RICHMOND,
Forestville, N. Y.

*[The above formerly published in the Baptist Register.]*

Having used the Grape Wine in my practice, manufactured by Dea. E. Fay & Sons, at Salem ⋈ Roads, I can recommend it as being superior, to be used in case of sickness, to that imported, in consequence of its not containing any alcohol.
CHAUNCEY FULLER,
Ripley, 29th April, 1843.

We hereby certify that Dea. E. Fay & Sons furnish the purest and most suitable Wine for Sacramental purposes, that can be found in our country. The Churches in the vicinity have found this out, and supply themselves accordingly. No alcohol is used in making it, and we are confident that the publication of the above notice would do the public a special benefit. It is preferable also, for medicinal use, to all other.

A. W. GRAY,
Pastor of the Congregational Church, Portland, N. Y.

J. E. CHAPIN,
Pastor of the M. E. Church, Portland, N. Y.

JONATHAN WILSON,
Baptist Minister, North East, Pa.

CHARLES LA HATT,
Minister in Portland.

B. WALWORTH,
Physician and Surgeon, Fredonia, N. Y.

SQUIRE WHITE, M.D., do.

GEORGE LATHROP, M. D.

W. C. WOLCOTT, M. D.,
Salem ⋈ Roads, N. Y.

ASA PIERCE.

A. HINCKLEY.

JA'S DELVIN.

The first juice that Deacon Elijah Fay, founder and deacon of the First Portland Baptist Church, made was used for medicinal and sacramental purposes. This is an 1840s handbill with testimonials from pastors and doctors certifying that Fay's juice was pure and without alcohol.

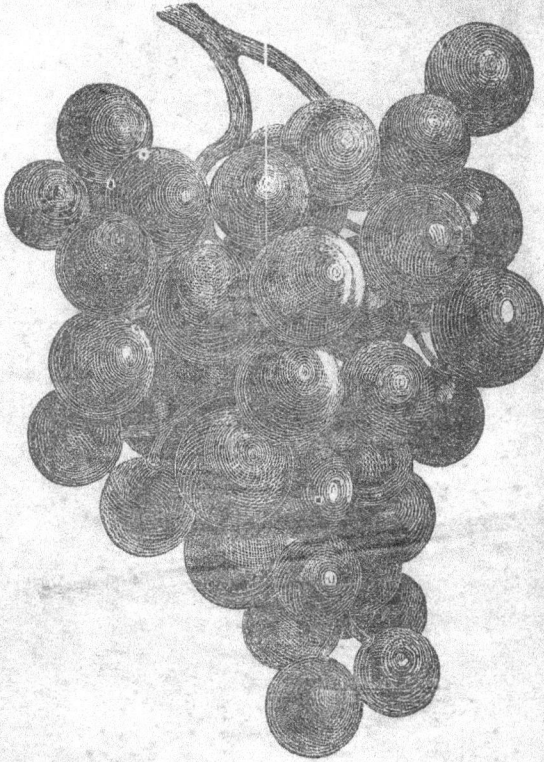

# FAY'S
# GRAPES,

CULTIVATED

AND PUT UP AT

# BROCTON,
## Chautauqua County, N. Y.

Elijah Fay established the first winery in 1830. The wine was made from Isabella and Catawba grapes. There was about 10 gallons made for medicinal and sacramental purposes. Gradually the little vineyard grew to produce 300 to 500 gallons per year. This was the first grape label used in Chautauqua County shortly after Salem Cross Roads's name was changed to Brocton.

RESIDENCE OF CAPT J. BUTLER, BROCTON, CHAUTAUQUA CO., N.Y.

GREEN HOUSES AND RESIDENCE OF G. E. RYCKMAN, BROCTON, CHAUTAUQUA CO., N.Y.

The Brocton Wine Cellars Winery was established 1859. These are lithographs of the winery and G. E. Ryckman residence and greenhouse as it appears in the 1867 *Chautauqua County Atlas*. Elijah Fay constructed his log cabin on this site, which was the first residence in Brocton. His son-in-law then built this elegant brick home. The home is still standing and is a private residence.

Ryckman, Day and Company was created in 1868 from the original G. E. Ryckman Brocton Wine Cellars. When this company took over, they purchased 24,000 gallons of wine from the former owners. By 1870, some 45,000 gallons of wine were made and in 1871, about 42,000 gallons. The varieties of grapes that were used were Catawba, Isabella, Concord, Clinton, Iona, and Delaware. Champagne and Brandy were also made in this superior winery. This is a pre-1900 Ryckman, Day and Company envelope.

The beautiful brick Ryckman Wine Cellars was built across Main Street from the Ryckman home and farm. It was a three-story building that produced superior wine. It was established in 1859 and incorporated in 1905. The building burned down in 1908.

Lakeshore Wine Company sold certificates of capital stock in the company. This certificate was for 10 shares worth $100 each that were purchased by Clinton Fay in 1865. T. Judson was the president of the company at that time with J. B. Fay as secretary.

Early local wines could be bought by the gallon or by the case. This is a list with prices of the Brocton wines from Brocton Wine Cellars around 1890. Their choices of wines were port, sherry, Catawba, claret, burgundy, and Diana. The most expensive were the J. S. Old port "60," their oldest reserve wine; D. G. sherry "60," their oldest reserve sherry; and Diana "62," which was a delicious wine. Each of those wines was a pricey $30 per case or $10 a gallon.

PRICE LIST OF

## BROCTON WINES

| PORT | Per case 12 full qts. | Per gal. |
|---|---|---|
| J. S. Old Port "60" | $30 00 | $10 00 |
| Fine Old Port "70" | 18 00 | 6 00 |
| Brocton Port "76" | 12 00 | 4 00 |
| White Port "78" | 12 00 | 4 00 |
| Sunnyside Port "84" | 9 00 | 3 00 |
| Concord Port, 10 yrs. old | 6 00 | 2 00 |

| SHERRY | | |
|---|---|---|
| D. G. Sherry "60" | 30 00 | 10 00 |
| Fine Old Sherry "72" | 18 00 | 6 00 |
| Sherry "82" | 10 00 | 3 00 |
| Sherry, 10 yrs. old | 6 00 | 2 00 |

| CATAWBA | | |
|---|---|---|
| Dry Catawba "80" | 10 00 | 3 00 |
| Sweet Catawba "80" | 10 00 | 3 00 |
| Dry Catawba, 10 yrs. old | 6 00 | 2 00 |
| Sweet Catawba, 10 yrs. old | 6 00 | 2 00 |

| CLARET | | |
|---|---|---|
| Claret "80" | 8 00 | 2 50 |
| Claret, 10 yrs. old | 6 00 | 2 00 |

| BURGUNDY | | |
|---|---|---|
| Burgundy "76" | 12 00 | 4 00 |

| DIANA | | |
|---|---|---|
| Diana "62" a delicious wine | 30 00 | 10 00 |

## A Pure Wine

is as much a natural beverage as Tea or Coffee; we guarantee all Brocton Wines to be the pure juice of the grape.

Our efforts have always been to produce wine that will stand the test, in purity, bouquet, body and flavor, of a comparison with those, not only of America, but of Europe as well; the result is shown in our gradually increasing trade each year, wholly on the merits of the product.

We especially recommend our Port Wines for invalids and persons in delicate health.

Our Dry Wines are good appetizers and will aid digestion if drank with meals.

Pure Brandy is distilled from the grape, we guarantee every gallon manufactured and sold by us to be absolutely pure.

All goods guaranteed under the Pure Food and Drugs Act, June 30, 1906.

| | Per case 12 full qts. | Per gal. |
|---|---|---|
| **DELAWARE** | | |
| Old Sweet Delaware "64" | $15.00 | $5.00 |
| **IONA** | | |
| Dry Iona "75," Choice | 18.00 | 6.00 |
| Sweet Iona "75," very fine | 18.00 | 6.00 |
| **NIAGARA** | | |
| Dry Niagara "83" | 10.00 | 3.00 |
| Sweet Niagara "83" | 10.00 | 3.00 |
| **SALEM** | | |
| Salem "70," excellent | 24.00 | 8.00 |
| **TOKAY** | | |
| Tokay | 10.00 | 3.00 |
| **COMMUNION WINE** | | |
| Red Communion Wine | 6.00 | 2.00 |
| Altar Wine, white | 6.00 | 2.00 |
| **BRANDY** | | |
| Extra Old Grape Brandy | 36.00 | 12.00 |
| Fine Old Grape Brandy | 20.00 | 7.00 |
| Pure Grape Brandy | 12.00 | 4.00 |
| **WHISKEY** | | |
| Fine Old Rye | 15.00 | 5.00 |
| Fine Old Bourbon | 15.00 | 5.00 |

All goods in cases of 24 full pints, 50 cents per case extra.

The winery's prices were comparable after the beginning of the 20th century. This is a price list of Ryckman Wines a year before the winery burned. Their varieties of wine were different having Delaware, Iona, Niagara, Salem, Tokay, communion wine, brandy, and whiskey. The most expensive was the Extra Old Grape brandy selling for $36 per case or $12 per gallon.

The grape farm workers were responsible for growing and harvesting fine grapes that supplied the wineries. Women and hired men worked together. Women harvested while hired men did the heavy work on the farms. Here is an early photograph of grape harvest time. Women would pick the grapes into the baskets and the men would pack them on the wagons and take them to wineries or shipyards to be shipped.

Families worked together in the vineyards harvesting the grapes. This is a c. 1910 postcard showing a husband, wife, and child picking and packing grapes. With the amount of grapes on the vine, it must have been a very good productive year.

Once the grapes were picked, they were taken to a packinghouse. Workers then packed the grapes for shipping to markets or to wineries. People came from all over the county to earn money working in grape harvesting. Quite often, this was an opportunity to visit relatives as well as to earn money. This is a 1903 photograph taken by the Portland Packing House. As written on the back of this photograph, from back to front, are Mrs. Ince of Portland; Estella Fitzpatrick of Louisiana, Missouri; Fran Billings of Portland; Mirna Beebe of Titusville; Mrs. Clarence Arnold of Portland; Martin Peterson of Jamestown; George Fuller of Portland; Elva Hargraves of Chautauqua Hill; Libbie Anderson of Pittsfield, Pennsylvania; Mary Emerson of Grand Valley, Pennsylvania; Mrs. Charles Fralick of Portland; David Quist of Jamestown; Charlie Fralick of Portland; Mr. White of Fredonia; David McGregor of Portland; and Ralph Fuller of Portland.

Grape support industries were established in the town and village. Crandall Panel Company of Brocton was an important industry. This company was established by Jay E. Crandall, who was born in Brocton on September 22, 1860. He attended local public schools then started working in commercial enterprises. In 1887, he established this business and began the manufacture of grape baskets. In 1903, he became associated as a partner with L. H. Skinner and added to his basket factory the equipment to make veneer panels. This is a postcard showing the business at its heyday.

Loading Grapes at Brocton, N. Y.

This 1915 postcard shows men loading splint or two quart baskets of grapes into boxcars to be sent to market. It was a lot of work to get the grapes from the vineyard to market. However people in cities enjoyed the delicious flavor of these fresh Concord grapes.

Naboth Grape Juice Factory, Brocton, N. Y.

In the early 1900s, there were two grape juice companies in Brocton competing against one another for grapes to supply the wine industry: Naboth Grape Juice Factory and Brocton Fruit Products. The largest of the grape juice factories was the Naboth Grape Juice Factory. It was located on Central Avenue near the Pennsylvania and Nickel Plate and Lake Shore Railroads and established in 1903. The office was located in the State Bank building in the village of Brocton. The 25 workers could make up to 200,000 gallons of juice per year. The company also had eight traveling salesmen on the road. The company only sold wholesale. The president of the company was F. C. Lewis, E. C. Edmonds was the vice president, and C. A. Putman was the secretary-treasurer. The other juice company was Brocton Fruit Products, which was established in 1880, and then again in 1900 by C. W. Green Jr. It was located on West Avenue in Brocton at the present site of the Little League Field. This is a c. 1915 postcard of the Naboth Grape Juice Factory.

The Paul DeLaney Company processed and preserved local fruits such as grape juice and apple butter. It was located in an E. J. Bailey-built building on Peerless Street north of the railroad tracks. It was a very successful business owned by Paul DeLaney. There is no published reason, but in 1925, DeLaney was convicted and sent to jail for fraud. His company then folded, and the Brocton village board needed an occupant for the empty building. Negotiations were held with Huntley Manufacturing Company from Silver Creek to move into the building, but it was determined to be too costly. Therefore the Brocton village board held a special election on July 20, 1925, to vote on a proposition to issue bonds not to exceed $15,000 to help defray the expense of moving Huntley Manufacturing Company to Brocton if it purchased the building. The vote was in favor, 119 to 17. The company moved to Brocton and remained until the 1960s.

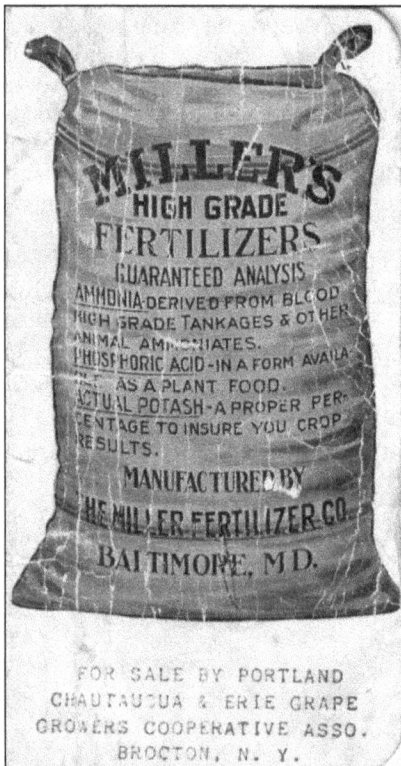

This is a little pocket notebook advertising Miller's High Grade Fertilizers, manufactured by the Miller Fertilizer Company of Baltimore, Maryland. It was purchased and used by the grape farmers. The fertilizer was for sale at the Chautauqua and Erie Grape Growers Cooperative Association in Brocton.

### ⇛ Certificate ✕ of ✕ Stock. ⇚

No. 158

## CHAUTAUQUA GRAPE GROWERS' SHIPPING ASSOCIATI

This is to certify that _____ Burton _____ of

_____ of _____ Portland _____, Chautauqua Cou

New York, is entitled to One Share of the Capital Stoc

"The Chautauqua Grape Growers' Shipping Association."

This Certificate of Stock is transferable only by and with the consent o

Board of Directors of the Association, and subject to the

ditions of the articles of associations and the by-laws th

_____ Pre

Dated _____ Sept 1 188_ _____ Sec

Chautauqua Grape Growers' Shipping Association sold stock certificates for ownership into the company. They were very large and successful shippers of grapes. In later years, the company branched out producing their own line of grape products.

81

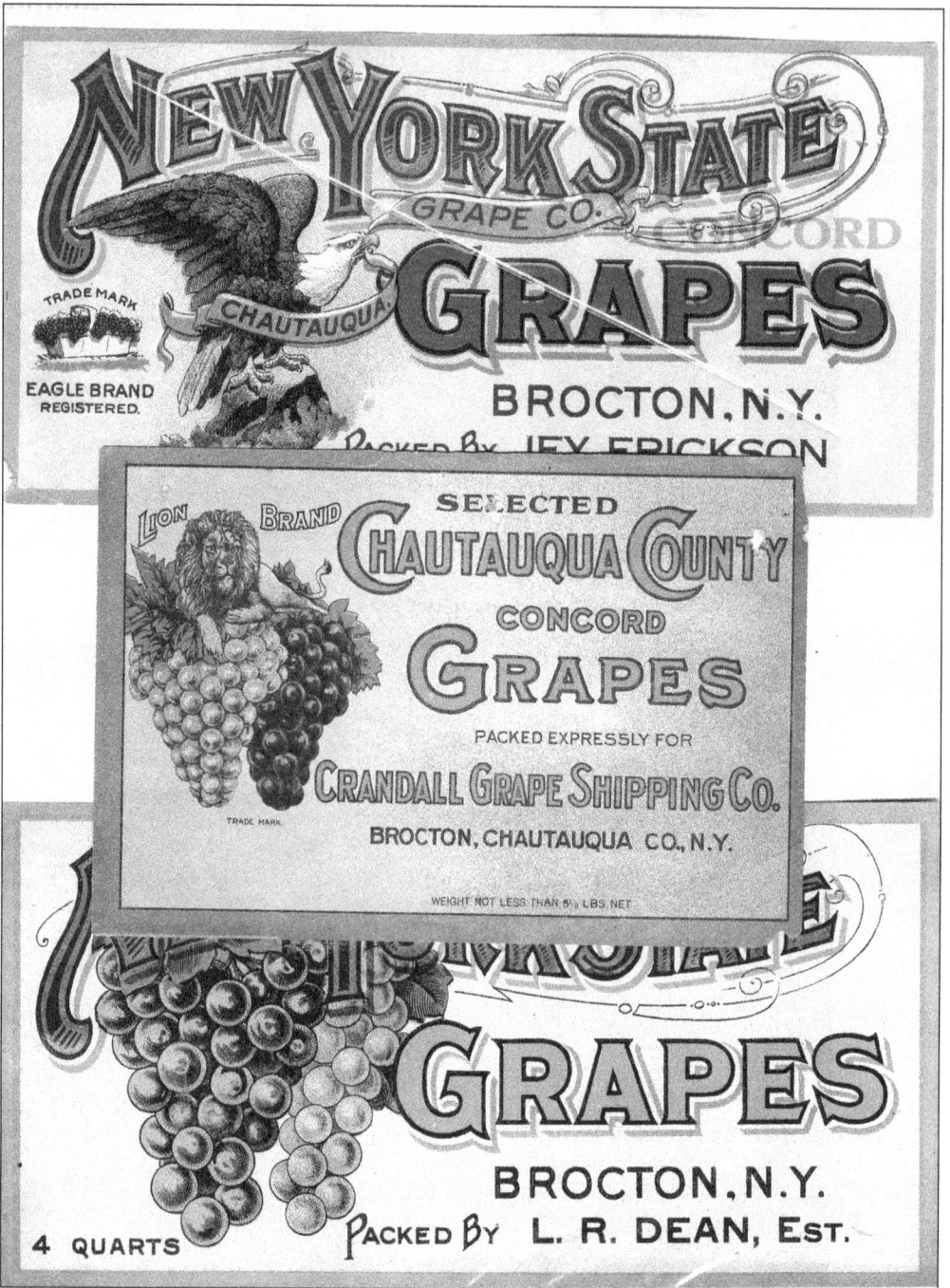

Grape packing companies attached grape labels to splint wood baskets. Each company had their own style and design, and they were all very colorful. Here are three labels. From top to bottom the packers were Jey Erickson, Crandall Packing Company, and L.R. Dean, all from Brocton.

| CONTENTS | ALCOHOL BY VOLUME |
|---|---|
| 4/5 Quart | 19 % |

## *Gilt Edge*

REG. U.S.    PAT. OFF.

MEDIUM          SWEET

## *American Sherry*

BOTTLED BY
*Brocton Wine Cellars, Inc.*
*Brocton, New York.*

TAX PAID BY STAMPS AFFIXED TO CASE

---

## OLD BROCTON
### BRAND

| Contents | | Alcohol by Volume |
|---|---|---|
| 4/5 Quart | | 19% |

## *American Tokay*

BOTTLED BY
**BROCTON WINE CELLARS, Inc.**
**BROCTON, NEW YORK**

---

| CONTENTS | ALCOHOL BY VOLUME |
|---|---|
| 4/5 Quart | 12 % |

## *Gilt Edge*

REG. U.S.    PAT. OFF.

## *American Sauterne*

BOTTLED BY
*Brocton Wine Cellars, Inc.*
*Brocton, New York.*

TAX PAID BY STAMPS AFFIXED TO CASE

---

Wine, juice, and jelly labels were also very colorful. Here are three different wine labels from the Brocton Wine Cellars: American Tokay, sherry, and sauterne. While they are not very colorful, they are elegant like the wine that was bottled. This is not the same wine company as in the 1850s.

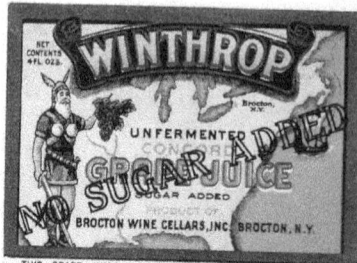

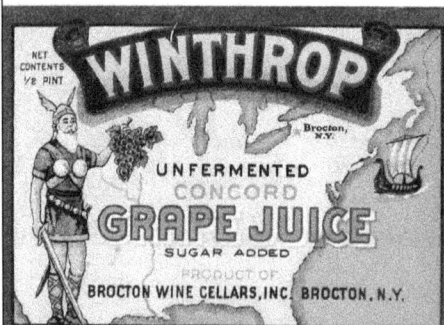

Brocton Wine Cellars also bottled unfermented sweetened and unsweetened grape juice under the label of Winthop. The label states the juice was pasteurized. Also note that one label reads that the juice was bottled by the National Grape Corporation in Brocton. In 1933, Jacob (Jake) Kaplan from New York City purchased C and E Grape Cooperative for its wine production. However wine making did not make a profit so Kaplan changed to grape products. Under his ownership, the company changed names several times, from C. and E. Grape Products Corporation, to Brocton Wine Cellars, to National Grape Corporation, until it merged with Welch's in 1945.

During the 1930s and early 1940s, the company owned by Kaplan bottled juice and labeled it for other companies around the country. O. V. Sharp from Portland was the supervisor in charge of production. Here are some of the 50 independent companies that the juice was bottled and labeled for.

In 1945, under Jacob (Jake) Kaplan's unique plan, the formation of the National Cooperative occurred. This was a grower-owner business that purchased National Grape Corporation from Kaplan. Kaplan had a problem. He had just purchased the Welch's plant in Nashville, Tennessee, which was in competition with the National Grape Cooperative Association that he had sold his business to. He wanted to buy Welch's in Brocton and had a meeting with Paul Welch in order to do so. He offered the chairmanship of Welch's grape juice company to Paul Welch and he accepted. This postcard shows the Brocton Welch's plant in 1963. The plant closed in the 1970s and was torn down in 2005 and 2006.

Huntley Grape Juice Plant, (World's Largest), Brocton, N. Y.

Huntley Manufacturing Company's grape juice plant was the world's largest and located in Brocton on the north side of the railroad tracks east of Vineyard. This business card shows the plant in its prime as well as the types and prices.

# Various Blends of Huntley's Grape Juice

PRESSED AND BLENDED FROM FIRST QUALITY GRAPES AND
GUARANTEED FREE FROM ALL IMPURITIES

### AS MADE BY

## HUNTLEY MANUFACTURING COMPANY

Established 1853

### BROCTON, Chautauqua Co., New York

| TYPES | | PRICES | | |
|---|---|---|---|---|
| REISLING | Dry White Type | 10 GALLONS | - | $30.00 |
| SAUTERN | Light Dry White | | | |
| TOKAY | Medium Sweet White | 15 " | - | 40.00 |
| MUSCATEL | Sweet Light Amber | | | |
| SHERRY | Dry Amber Type | 25 " | - | 65.00 |
| MADERIA | Heavy Sweet Amber | 50 " | - | 110.00 |
| CATAWBA | Heavy Sweet White | | | |
| CLARET | Tart Red Type | Delivered in Quartered Oak Kegs, | | |
| BURGUNDY | Heavy Tart Red | Via. Railway Express Agency. | | |
| PORT | Sweet Red Type | All Charges Prepaid. | | |

### Direct from the ORIGINAL HUNTLEY CELLARS

Represented by

This side lists Huntley Manufacturing Company's wines. In the mid-1960s, the business closed its doors. In a storage shed on the property were 5,000 five-gallon crock jugs with handle. They had black, brown, or all white bottoms with white necks and handles. These were used to store the grape juice at Huntley's. They sold for 20¢ a piece. They can be seen today in antique auctions or shops.

87

## Special Announcement---

You are cordially invited to enjoy the whole day at

## BROCTON, NEW YORK

### " Where The Good Blue Grape Grows "

See the vast acres of Vineyards hanging with the Lucious Chautauqua Blue Grapes.

Visit the largest producing Grape Juice Plant in the World. See the production of Grape Juice, from the grape to the finished product.

Enjoy a 40 mile auto tour along Lake Erie Shore. Entire tour right thru the heart of the FAMOUS CHAUTAUQUA VINEYARDS.

## Special Excursion

### PENNSYLVANIA RAIL ROAD

Leaving Pittsburgh September 19th. and October 11th. at 11:30 P. M. arriving Brocton at 6:00 A. M. next day. Leaving Brocton for return to Pittsburgh, at 12:30 the same day.

### Round Trip Fare $5.25

Tourism abounded in town during grape harvesting time. This is an advertisement for a special excursion on the Pennsylvania Railroad. The round trip fare cost $5.25 and left Pittsburgh, Pennsylvania, on September 19 and October 11 at 11:30 p.m., arriving in Brocton the following morning at 6:00 a.m., and returning to Pittsburgh at 12:30 p.m. the same day. Visitors could tour the vineyards, the grape juice plants, and take automobile tours along the lakeshore. Other visitors also came into town by automobile or trolley to enjoy and sample the luscious grapes that were grown.

# *Eight*

# SCHOOLS

In 1810, the first school was built on Capt. James Dunn's property in the town. It was a log cabin that was located on Webster Road just west of Cemetery Avenue and had six or seven students. The teacher was Anna Eaton. A few years later another school was built on the corner of Munson and Webster Roads. Later another school was established on Webster Road about a mile east of the junction with Highland Avenue. Some other early school districts were located on Woleben Road and Pecor Street and also on Fay Street in the hamlet. The first school in the village stood on the east side of Slippery Rock Creek and the north side of Main Street. School District No. 6 was built of rough board with a board chimney in 1819. Miss Kimball was the teacher. The school burned down the same day that it opened. Another school building was soon erected on the same location. Then a larger school was built in 1824, but again burned down a short time after opening. Another school was again built to replace it.

By 1887, the population of Brocton had increased to where it became apparent that a larger school was needed for the village. The Brocton Union School was built in 1887, and then enlarged in 1899, 1907, and 1924. It was used until the Brocton Central School was built in 1939. The building is now shared by the Brocton Fire Department and the Community Youth Center.

Brocton Central School has since serviced the community. The school has seen many additions including a new high school gym and pool. The latest addition was completed in 2005. It is a school that the community is very proud of.

OLD STONE SCHOOL HOUSE,

The old stone schoolhouse, School District No. 3, was located on Webster Road in West Portland. It is not known when it was in use. However a new log cabin school was built across the road from the stone schoolhouse in 1810–1811. The new school had a small door and four pane windows. In the school there was a Dutch fireplace with a hole in the roof to let out the smoke. The teacher was Augustine Klumph. The location was inconvenient for the settlers and it closed after one year.

This is the monument that was erected by former students of Portland School District No. 7. It was located on the northern portion of Pecor Street. The school was a log house and was erected in 1819.

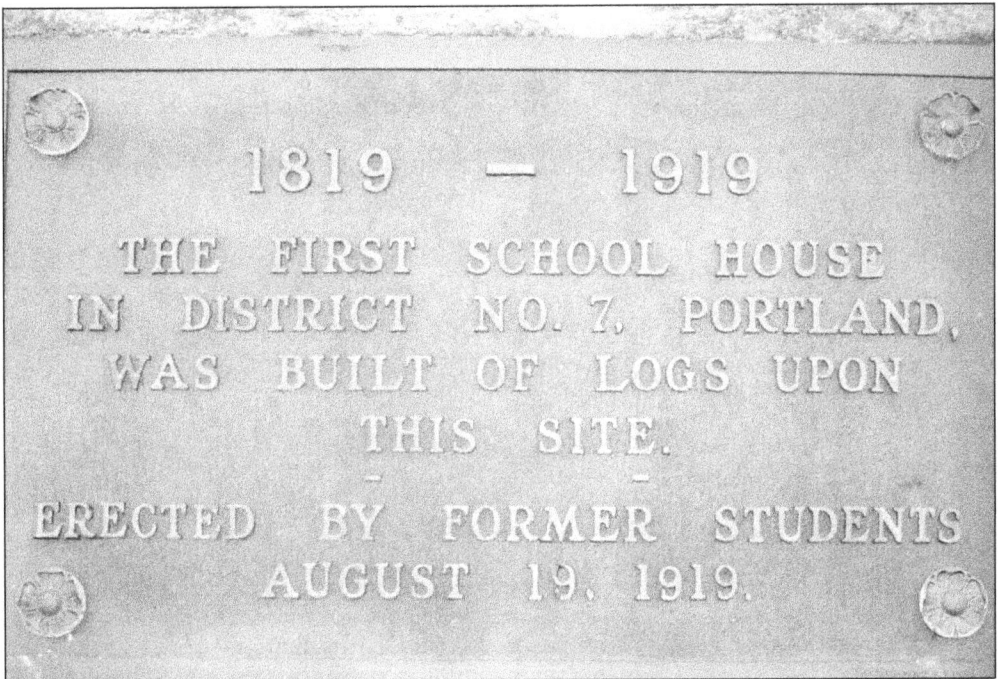

1819 — 1919
THE FIRST SCHOOL HOUSE
IN DISTRICT NO. 7, PORTLAND,
WAS BUILT OF LOGS UPON
THIS SITE.

ERECTED BY FORMER STUDENTS
AUGUST 19, 1919.

The monument remains a reminder to all students of the hardships the early settlers went through in order to obtain an education. Many family members of the students at this school come to visit this monument as a reminder of their ancestors.

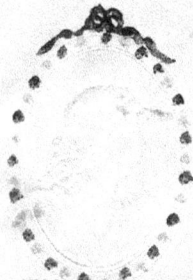

The teacher's pledge reads as follows: "United We Stand. We, Members of the Teacher's Class in Portland, promise to abstain from Intoxicating Drinks as a Beverage, including Wine and Cider, and also from the use of Tobacco, Tea and Coffee; and to use our influence in favor of all moral and intellectual improvements." The names below are Charles Burton, Charles Case, James Hulburt, Emmet Kesslar, Darwin Mason, Franklin Johnson, Westwood Case, William Harris, Wesley Felton, Allen Mason, Francis Pecor, James Skinner, Porter Haines, Chester Burton, Flora Brown, Narcissa Laine, Clarissa Laine, Lavantia Case, Sarah Lilly, Mary Driggs, Frances Wade, and Fidelia Harris. It was dated November 11, 1853.

This is a Brocton Union School graduation exercises program from June 24, 1892. The program consisted of an opening with a prayer, musical selections, essays, recitations, presentation of diplomas and the good bye. Teachers and students participated.

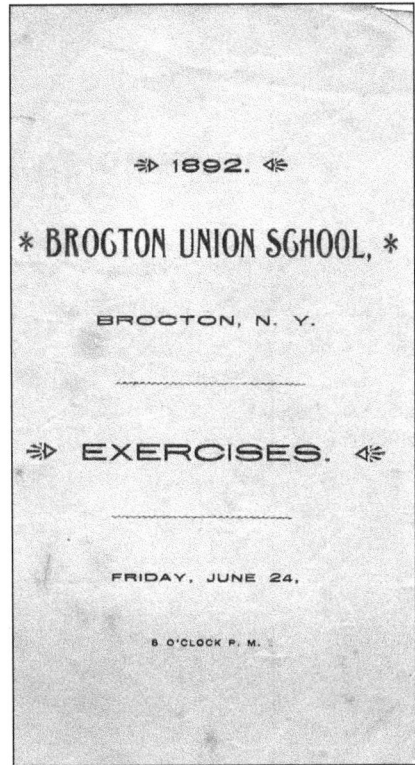

⇒ 1892. ⇐

## * BROCTON UNION SCHOOL, *

BROCTON, N. Y.

⇒ EXERCISES. ⇐

FRIDAY, JUNE 24,

8 O'CLOCK P. M.

**PROGRAMME—PART FIRST.**

1. Chorus. - - "Boat Song,"
   BY THE SCHOOL.
   **PRAYER.**
2. Salutatory,
   HERBERT SWETLAND.
3. Silvery Stars, - - Carl Bohm.
   RUBY BREEN.
4. Recitation, - "The Whistling Regiment,"
   HELEN ROBERTS.
5. Vocal Solo, - "He's Got the Money, Too,"
   BESSIE MOSS.
6. Dairy Maids' Drill.
7. Anchored, - - Samuel Cowan,
   EVA HALL.
8. Essay - - An Aim in Life,
   LYDA FURMAN.
9. Chorus and Solo. - "Voices of Nature,"
   PRIMARY DEPARTMENT.
10. Marsch. - Alexis Hollaender,
    AURA LOWELL.
    Tableau. The Reaper and the Flowers.

**PROGRAMME—PART SECOND.**

1. Recitation, - - A Short Speech,
   EDDIE LA DUE.
2. In Old Madrid, - H. Trotere,
   JENNIE MARTIN.
3. Dumb Bell Drill With Anvil Chorus.
4. Recitation, - Flag of the Rainbow,
   BLANCHE HANLEY.
5. Mill Clock, - - Rafael Joseffy,
   LYDA FURMAN.
6. Sunflower Concert,
   (a) Sunflower Chorus.
   (b) Solo and Chorus.
   Presentation of Diplomas.
7. Chorus,
   GOOD BYE.

The order of the program is shown here. The evening must have been very entertaining with the diverse form of talents that performed.

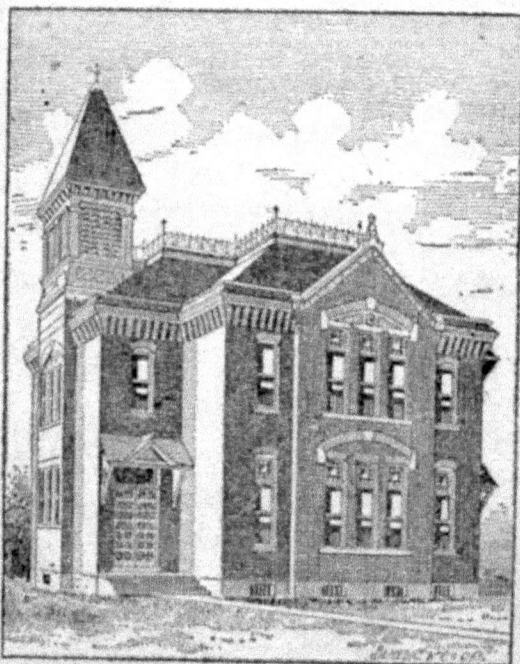

**BROCTON UNION SCHOOL**

**AND ACADEMY.**

**Under the Visitation of the Regents.**

The Fall Term of 13 weeks will open
September 4th, 1893.

An informational booklet was printed for the Brocton Union School and Academy's 1893 school year. It included the location of the school, the advantages, library and apparatus, regulations, calendar for the school year, room and board expenses, and the courses of study, including the classical course, the academic course, and the English course. On the board of education was E. C. Edmunds, John Skinner, R. A. Hall, Augusta Blood, Dr. Swetland, O. L. Porter, and E. P. Harris. The faculty consisted of George Hanley, Katherine Barber, Anna May Paschke, and Lyda Furman.

94

School District No. 9 was located on Lake Avenue south of the train tracks. It was a lovely one-story brick building with a school bell dome. This was also known as the Burton School, as most of the students were members of the Burton family. The school is no longer standing.

School District No. 10 school was located on Fay Street in the hamlet of Portland. Also known as the Union School, it was a grand two-story building with a school bell dome. After the building ceased being used as a school, the Portland Grange owned it for many years. It then became a lovely private residence.

The Brocton Union School was a beautiful building located near the center of the village. Above is a postcard of the school that was postmarked in 1911. The card was published by the Rossiter Drug Company in Brocton. Seen below, the postcard postmarked in 1923 shows the school when it was renamed Brocton High School. The building looks the same but the trees are mature.

School District No. 7 was located on Pecor Street in Portland. Here is a photograph of a reunion held in a nice clapboard school built on the site of the original log cabin. Looking at the people in attendance, one might wonder if any of them did attend the original log school.

VIEW FROM THE EAST, CENTRAL SCHOOL OF THE TOWNSHIPS OF PORTLAND, STOCKTON AND POMFRET

The community was proud when the Brocton Central School was planned and built. The central school encompasses the town of Portland and portions of Stockton and Pomfret. This late 1930s postcard shows the architect's drawing of the proposed school.

Brocton Central School, Brocton, N.Y.

This 1939 real-photo postcard shows the beautiful school completed. The school has grown to about twice its size. With all the additions, the building has still kept its character.

98

# Nine

# CHURCHES

Churches have always been an important part of the town and village. Although there was no formal religion, the earliest settlers held religious meetings whenever it was possible. The first religious meeting was held at Capt. James Dunn's home in 1810. Rev. John Spencer led the service. Spencer continued to preach in town occasionally but traveling ministers led formal services usually on a weekday evening for the following three or four years. In 1814, the first formal religious service was held in a log tavern house. In 1818, Spencer was instrumental in the formation of the Congregational church. There were 18 original members. In 1868, there was a difference of opinion in the church polity. Some parishioners wanted the church to become a Presbyterian church, but others did not. Those parishioners then split away from the church. The Congregational church is still active.

The second church to be established in Portland was the Methodist Episcopal church in 1816. The first member was William Dunham. The original Methodist church was located in the hamlet of Portland. In 1853, a portion of the congregation united with a group of Methodists on Harmon Hill to form a Methodist church in Salem Cross Roads.

The third church formed was the First Baptist Church of Portland in 1819. There were 11 original members. In 1842, the West Portland Baptist Church was established to better serve those parishioners on the western part of town. It was first a branch of the First Baptist Church of Portland, but then became a separate church in 1842.

Universalist Church and Society was created in 1821 by 14 original members. A year later, the church was officially formed. This group met in private homes then schoolhouses for their worship but now is no longer worshiping in town.

The Roman Catholic church had about 30 members in the 1870s. Most were Irish descendents.

The Lutheran church was formed in the town in the 1872. The congregation was made up of mostly Swedish descendents.

There are several other churches in the town. The Free Methodist Church has an active congregation and was formed in 1934. There is also a Seventh Day Adventist Church that was formed in 1955 and remains active. Finally another Baptist congregation built a church by Lake Erie.

## DONATION VISIT.

*You are respectfully Invited to attend a Donation Visit, to be given for the benefit of Rev. Peter Burroughs, at his residence in Portland, on the afternoon and evening of Wednesday, April 28th, 1858.*

### Committee of Arrangements, for Afternoon:

| | |
|---|---|
| JAS. HALL & LADY, | R S MORRISON & LADY, |
| WM. MARTIN " " | ASA BLOOD " " |
| A EATON " " | R REYNOLDS " " |
| L. FAY " " | DAVID DUNN " " |
| R. MOSIER " " | J. CORRELL " " |
| C. S. BURTON " " | H STEVER " " |

JOSEPH CORRELL, *Receiver.*

### Committee of Arrangements, for Evening:

ALFRED ELLIS & LADY,
WM. HARRIS " "
F. CALDWELL " "

| | |
|---|---|
| Mr. HOSEA CRANDALL, | Miss CAROLINE WEST, |
| " EDWIN MILLER, | " EDDY FAY, |
| " HENRY COLT. | " OLIVA DEDRICK, |
| " JACOB HIPWELL | " SARAH MILLER, |
| " FRANK PECOR, | " ANN GRANT, |
| " ALFRED BURTON, | " ELIZABETH ELMORE. |
| " WM. DEDRICK, | " MALVINA HELSY, |
| " LUDLOW OGDEN, | " C. VAN LOOVAN, |
| " WM. JUDSON, | " HELEN JONES, |

ADDISON BARRINGER, *Receiver,*
ALFRED BURTON, *Secretary.*

Ministers serving the congregations of early Portland received their pay through donations from parishioners. The congregation was invited to attend a donation visit held on a weekday afternoon and evening. This is an invitation to attend a donation visit for the benefit of Rev. Peter Burroughs in Portland on Wednesday, April 28, 1858.

In Centerville on March 6, 1857, there was a donation party for the benefit of Rev. L. F. Laine. There were both afternoon and evening sessions with different committees for each. The receiver was Chester Burton. On the back of the invitation it is written that Mary Ann Burton was present.

## DONATION PARTY.

*You are respectfully invited to attend a*

### DONATION VISIT,

FOR THE

### Benefit of Rev. L. F. Laine,

AT HIS RESIDENCE

IN CENTERVILLE,

ON

FRIDAY AFTERNOON AND EVE., MARCH 6, 1857.

#### COMMITTEE FOR AFTERNOON.

| | | |
|---|---|---|
| Franklin Pecor & Lady. | J. E. Harris & Lady, | Timothy Judson & Lady. |
| Warren Couch " | John S. Coon " | Lincoln Fay " |

#### COMMITTEE FOR EVENING.

| | | |
|---|---|---|
| Miss Ann Couch, | Miss Maria R. Burton, | Mr. John W. Bowdish. |
| Mary L. Pecor, | Louisa H. Burton, | O. L. Ogden, |
| Freedom Harris, | Mary F. Churchill, | Jas. Ogden, |
| Frank A. Wade, | Kate Judd, | Warren Couch. |
| Bethia Taylor, | Jane Judd, | Geo. Arnold, |
| Emily ..ouch | Mary A Driggs, | Hilal Skinner. |
| Eda Fay, | Lucy C. Hadden, | A. J. Skinner, |
| Victoria Peck, | Lodolska M. Hall, | Jerome Laine. |
| Celestia Peck, | Mr Frank Pecor, | Jay Morrison. |
| Eliza Simons. | Wm. E. Harris, | Jacob Hipwell. |
| Sarah A. Skinner, | Salmon Burton, | Jas. A Skinner, |
| Julia Bacon. | Milton M. R'ce, | Jas. W. Skinner, |
| Susan Bacon, | Alfred B. Rice, | Chas. W. Burton. |
| Lydia J. R'ce, | West W. Case, | |

RECEIVER, - - - CHESTER W. BURTON.

This February 11, 1859, donation party for the benefit of Rev. W. R. Connolly had both afternoon and evening sessions. It was held at the parsonage and D. G. Goodrich was the treasurer and clerk. The committee for the evening session was larger, however, no refreshments were served in the evening.

**Donation Visit.**

You are respectfully invited to attend a Donation Visit for the Benefit of

Rev. W. R. CONNOLLY

TO BE HELD AT THE PARSONAGE,

Brocton, Friday Feb. 11th, 1859, Afternoon and Evening.

**Committee of Arrangements for Afternoon.**

. B. Haywood & Lady,     J. P. Chamberlain & Lady

COMMITTEE FOR EVENING.

G. E. Ryckman,     Miss Sarah Skinner,
R. S. Morrison,     Miss Eliza Simons,
Ahira Hall,     Miss Sarah Haight,
James Skinner,     Miss Lucy Ryckman.

No Refreshments in the Evening.

D. G. GOODRICH, Treasurer and Clerk.

1885,     1890.

First Baptist Church,

Brocton, N. Y.

REV. W. C. WILTSE,

PASTOR.

SIXTH ANNUAL DONATION

For the Pastor.

The First Baptist Church of Brocton held its sixth annual donation party for its pastor, Rev. W. C. Wiltse, on Wednesday evening, December 17, 1890, in the church parlors. This is a nice card invitation for the event.

The Portland Methodist Church is now a private residence. In 1985, a consolidation agreement was made between the Portland Methodist, Brocton Methodist, and Salem Lutheran Churches to form one body and worship in the largest of the three buildings, which was the Brocton Methodist Church. The Salem Lutheran and Portland Methodist buildings were sold.

The Brocton Methodist Church and parsonage is shown here in this 1906 postcard. The architecture is similar to the Portland Methodist Church. The sanctuary is built on a slant with curved pews. This allows the people sitting in the back pews to see the minister and vise versa. The two large stained glass windows are beautiful with colorful religious symbols adorning them in the glass. Capt. James Butler, a wealthy ship captain who lived in the village, donated one window. The other large stained glass window was donated by Mr. Porter, a minister. There are many other small stained glass windows and beautiful oak woodwork. The pipe organ is original to the building.

The other church that makes up the Tri-Church Parish is the Salem Lutheran Church. One Sunday a month, the congregation worships in the Lutheran Liturgy and the other three Sundays are in Methodist Liturgy. This photograph is a 1961 confirmation class of the Salem Lutheran Church. From left to right are (first row) William Schruise, Evelyn Dean Suppo, William Fox, and Patricia Judge Kurtz; (second row) Robert Richardson, Linda Johnson Janes, and Robert "Doc" Benjamin; (third row) district minister and pastor of First Lutheran Church of Jamestown Pastor Paul Westerberg, and lay minister of Salem Lutheran Church Carl Holt.

The Brocton Baptist Church is as beautiful today as it appears in this 1911 postcard. A parsonage was built shortly after this postcard was published. The church bells were tolled when there was a fire in town. The bells are located on the west side of the church on the corner of Fay and Main Streets in Brocton.

The West Portland Baptist Church is an extremely active church. When it was first started, the old stone schoolhouse was used as their place of worship. This brick structure was made from handmade bricks and completed in 1842. Today the original church is used for offices and meeting rooms, and connected to it is a new large, modern church.

## 1891.

This certifies that the holder hereof has paid twenty-five (25) cents as a donation towards the indebtedness and for the improvements of St. Patrick's Church, at Brocton, N. Y.

Rev. Jas. P. Lasher, *Rector*.

*N. B.—Please retain this ticket and if entitled to a present you will be notified.*

The early St. Patrick's Church held fund-raisers to benefit the congregation. This 1891 ticket stub certified that the holder paid 25¢ toward the indebtedness for improvements of the St. Patrick's Church. The holder would be notified if they had won a present.

Catholic parishioners built their small church on Pullman Street and named it St. Michael's because it was a mission of St. James Church in Westfield. In 1922, when this church became a parish, the name was changed to St. Patrick's Parish. On January 31, 1941, a fire destroyed the church. The bishop would not allow a new church be built on the property because the diocese did not have a clear title to it. Worship services were held in the hall and theater in Brocton on Sundays until 1944.

Father Early bought the present property on Central Avenue for $10,000 around 1930. The purchase price included the present rectory and one and a half acres of land. After the old church burned, a new church building was necessary. On July 22, 1943, the contracts were signed to build the present church. St. Patrick's Church was dedicated on July 11, 1944.

# Ten

# PORTLAND CENTENNIAL CELEBRATION

The town of Portland was prosperous in 1913. There were many farms, wineries, merchants, and plenty of jobs for residents. When the town was 100 years old, a grand celebration was planned. The Portland Centennial Committee was in charge of the festivities. An iron double arch was purchased from a French manufacturer and erected across the four corners of Main Street in the village of Brocton, which was the center of the activities. An electric sign that said Brocton hung from the arch. The four-day event was held August 5–8, 1913. All homes, as well as the hotels in town and neighboring communities, were open to house the visitors. Thirty trains on the Pennsylvania Nickel Plate and Lakeshore Railroad stopped each day in Brocton to bring and return visitors. The B. and L. E. Traction Company provided more than their usual hourly runs accommodating the guests. Automobiles were taken care of as well as hitching posts and sheds for teams of horses.

The program listed August 5 as the reception day, August 6 as old settlers day, August 7 as the fraternal day, and August 8 honored the firemen.

All factory whistles and church bells rang as the celebration started on Tuesday, August 5. Large crowds attended each day and it was deemed that it was a great social success.

Village residents purchased and built a double arch over the four corners of Brocton to celebrate the town's first 100 years. The total cost of construction was $1,300. The Village of Brocton contributed $300, and the remainder was raised through private donations. It was lit at night by 124 electric bulbs, and an electric sign reading Brocton hung in the center. The arch still stands and is on the National Register of Historic Places. The color lights are changed for holidays. Residents remain proud that the arch is the only one on Route 20.

This 1950s postcard shows the modern Brocton arch. It is painted dark green with white lights. In 1976, the arch was painted red, white, and blue with matching lights. At night, the arch remains a spectacular sight.

Anticipation ran high for Portland's Centennial Celebration. Here is a postcard advertising the event. The back is printed "There will be some familiar sights in your old home town. August 5–8, 1913."

The first day of the celebration was founder's day. There was a band concert, free street attractions, contests, a ball game, a reception for county officers, and a dance during the day. The press headquarters was located near the home of W. P. Scrivens. All the press was welcome.

There were other street attractions and booths. These women were advertising for Votes for Women.

Festive patriotic decorations adorned businesses, homes, and streets throughout the town. The St. Stephens Hotel opened its doors for guests and partygoers. Many flags and bunting were used for decoration. People were beginning to arrive for the festivities as seen on the balconies and around the hotel.

Crowds gathered for the weeklong celebration as this photograph shows. This view is at the four corners with crowds traveling down Lake Avenue. The beautiful decorations on the buildings and the arch can be seen.

At Vineyard, across the street from the Vineyard Hotel, a reception tent was set up to welcome those arriving by train. The small hotel was also well decorated.

The second day of the celebration was old settlers day. Some older town residents and early settlers's photographs were on a promotional centennial celebration postcard. Listed from left to right with their ages are (first row) David Benjamin, 84; David McGregor, 90; Otis Fay, 93; A. T. Mead, 90; and Manley Thayer, 87; (second row) Mortimer Francis, 84; Homer Skinner, 85; M. J. Munson, 86; and A. J. Skinner, 84. Descendants from several of these early settlers still reside in the town.

At 11:00 a.m. on Wednesday, an automobile parade was held. Those fortunate enough to own an automobile were encouraged to decorate it and drive it in the parade. They formed on Smith and Fay Streets in Brocton, then went through the village, up to the hamlet of Portland, then back, disbanding in Fay Street Park. This automobile is decorated in a patriotic theme.

About 40 automobiles participated in the parade. This automobile is beautifully decorated with flowers and vines and every part off the car is covered. The women look fashionable with their parasols open.

These girls look like they are having an enjoyable time. The decorations were very nice with stars on the hubcaps, pompoms, and garland. The color scheme was red, white, and blue.

PORTLAND IN 1800
GRINDING CORN IN STONE MORTAR
"EVERYBODY WORKED BUT FATHER"

At 3:00 p.m. on Wednesday there was another parade where $15 in prize money awarded. This combined the historical, grotesque, and industrial floats and units. An estimated 5,000 to 7,000 people attended on this day to view the parade. Many also stayed for the evening events. Jessie Farnham and family entered this historical float of a wigwam with a squaw grinding corn in an old stone mortar.

The manager of this historical float was O. Bennett. These were Native Americans on foot with pony drawing poles. The horse is beautifully decorated with fringe, bells, and feathers on his ears.

C. W. Wenborne entered an interesting float depicting a log cabin built in 1804. He placed the cabin on a decorated wagon. His horses were wearing appropriate decorations. As Wenborne was waiting for the parade to continue, he probably thought of how much the town modernized since the log cabin was used.

The crowds were present Wednesday to enjoy the events of the day. This photograph shows that many people were present in order to view the floats. Automobiles were finding it hard to find parking spaces.

"Hetchling and spinning 4,257 yards of linen cloth made." Carding and spinning wool was another popular float in the historical section of the parade. Mrs. Corell and Mrs. Barhite entered and rode on the float.

Brocton Wines entered a beautiful float decorated with grape vines, a wine vat, and barrels. This photograph was taken in front of their decorated business on Main Street.

Luther Ross Dean farms of Brocton entered an interesting float. The wagon was filled with their grape-labeled boxes and grape vines. Luther Dean and son, Alvin, rode on the float. The Dean's Victorian home was located on West Main Street in Brocton where the American Legion is today.

A. A. Fay of Portland entered a lovely decorated float. On the patriotically decorated wagon he displayed that he was a dealer of Lehigh Valley Company fruit juices.

Crandall Panel Company was proud to enter several floats in the parade. Their first float was titled "From Forest to the Finished Product." A four-horse team pulled a wagon with three huge logs.

Crandall Panel Company's second float was a four-horse team pulling a wagon with a house on it, including curtains and a flower box. This shows the continuity between the logs and the finished product.

Most of the merchants and farmers entered floats in the industrial portion of the parade. A big, but very pleasant, surprise occurred when about 30 automobiles loaded with Dunkirk merchants headed by the Lake City Band appeared at the parade and provided music.

J. F. Scott from the hamlet of Portland drove a decorated float in this event. It was titled "J. F. Scott Sells Everything to Eat & Wear." The wagon was adorned with bunting and displayed Melrose flour bags, which Scott sold. It appears that family and friends were riding on the wagon.

Ross Goldsmith, a hardware and plumbing merchant in the village of Brocton, showed new plumbing supplies on his float. His son is sitting in a new bathtub with a toilet beside it.

Decorated trucks with their wares also drove in the parade. This exhibit is a great delivery truck with patriotic bunting, flour bags, and a piece of furniture. The two gentlemen on the truck seem to be enjoying themselves.

This is a view of East Main Street with some of the floats traveling west. There were people everywhere. They were on the streets, on the porches, and in the automobiles. The flags and the bunting were so patriotic. It was almost unbelievable to see the large crowd that gathered to help a small town celebrate a 100-year birthday.

The last section of Wednesday's parade was the grotesque section. This band is not identified but sure look a little grotesque as they marched down the streets of town.

Thursday, August 7 was declared fraternal day. There were 16 fraternal and beneficiary societies in town. They invited neighboring societies to join them in the parade. Most of the societies that were invited participated. Here is A. T. Mead, age 90, in his carriage. He was honored as the oldest Odd Fellow in New York State. He sure looked proud.

Friday was fireman's day. It was a beautiful day and the crowds came early. There were 25 to 30 volunteer fire companies with decorated hose carts and many bands also marched. Here is a photograph of the marching bands as they paraded along the route.

The Citizen's Band of Brocton was always pleased to march and entertain with their professional sound. Here they are relaxing after their march. They are on West Main Street.

Citizens' Hose Company, Brocton, N. Y.

The members of the Citizen's Hose Company were very proud to march in their handsome uniforms. Here they are posed for a photograph prior to the parade. With most every town represented in the county, the local firemen knew that the parade and centennial was a success. There was one incident with the fireman that put a damper on the day's festivities. A group of rowdy drunks from out of town tried to ruin things at the dance, park, and police headquarters. They then went to the rear of Central House in the Hanley block and set one of the buildings on fire. It was quickly discovered and put out. However townspeople were very upset over the matter.

124

Here is the Brocton Citizen's Hose Company Jr. marching. They were the last marching unit of the entire celebration. These sons of Brocton were very proud to be part of the parade in a very important event. Furthermore to be the last to march in the weeklong event was considered an honor. The trolley was the only thing behind these marchers. The centennial was considered a huge success. It was talked about and remembered for many years. The committee hopes that the next centennial will be as great as this one.

The weeklong event had ended but crowds continued to linger around the center of the village. Many enjoyed friends and family that they had not seen in a very long time. But it was time to go back home and work. They had their souvenirs and memories that would be handed down from generation to generation. What a grand event!

# BIBLIOGRAPHY

Chazanof, William. *Welch's grape juice: From Corporation to Co-operative*. New York: Syracuse University Press, 1977.

*Chautauqua County Atlas*. William Stewart, 1867.

*Chautauqua County Atlas*. Beers Publication, 1881.

*International Magazine of Industry*. Stranton, Virginia: 1915.

Kurtz, E. T. & L.C. Smith. *Names and Places in Chautauqua County*. Self-published, 2001.

Kurtz, E. T. *Stories of Brocton*. Self-published, 1999.

Taylor, H. C. *Historical Sketches of the Town of Portland: Comprising also the Pioneer History of Chautauqua County, with Biographical Sketches of the Early Settlers*. Fredonia, NY: W. McKinstry & Son, 1873.

ACROSS AMERICA, PEOPLE ARE DISCOVERING
SOMETHING WONDERFUL. THEIR HERITAGE.

Arcadia Publishing is the leading local history publisher in the United States.
With more than 3,000 titles in print and hundreds of new titles released every
year, Arcadia has extensive specialized experience chronicling the history of
communities and celebrating America's hidden stories, bringing to life the people,
places, and events from the past. To discover the history of other communities
across the nation, please visit:

# www.arcadiapublishing.com

Customized search tools allow you to find regional history books about the town
where you grew up, the cities where your friends and family live, the town where
your parents met, or even that retirement spot you've been dreaming about.

* 9 7 8 1 5 3 1 6 3 0 9 8 0 *